THE NEW FOLGER LIBRARY SHAKESPEARE

Designed to make Shakespeare's great plays available to all readers, the New Folger Library edition of Shakespeare's plays provides accurate texts in modern spelling and punctuation, as well as scene-by-scene action summaries, full explanatory notes, many pictures clarifying Shakespeare's language, and notes recording all significant departures from the early printed versions. Each play is prefaced by a brief introduction, by a guide to reading Shakespeare's language, and by accounts of his life and theater. Each play is followed by an annotated list of further readings and by a "Modern Perspective" written by an expert on that particular play.

Barbara A. Mowat is Director of Research *emerita* at the Folger Shakespeare Library, Consulting Editor of *Shakespeare Quarterly*, and author of *The Dramaturgy of Shakespeare's Romances* and of essays on Shakespeare's plays and their editing.

Paul Werstine is Professor of English in the Graduate School and at King's University College at Western University. He is a general editor of the New Variorum Shakespeare and author of *Early Modern Playhouse Manuscripts and the Editing of Shakespeare*, as well as many papers and essays on the printing and editing of Shakespeare's plays.

Folger Shakespeare Library

The Folger Shakespeare Library in Washington, D.C., is a privately funded research library dedicated to Shakespeare and the civilization of early modern Europe. It was founded in 1932 by Henry Clay and Emily Jordan Folger, and incorporated as part of Amherst College in Amherst, Massachusetts, one of the nation's oldest liberal arts colleges, from which Henry Folger had graduated in 1879. In addition to its role as the world's preeminent Shakespeare collection and its emergence as a leading center for Renaissance studies, the Folger Shakespeare Library offers a wide array of cultural and educational programs and services for the general public.

EDITORS

BARBARA A. MOWAT
Director of Research emerita
Folger Shakespeare Library

PAUL WERSTINE
Professor of English
King's University College at the University of
Western Ontario, Canada

FOLGER SHAKESPEARE LIBRARY

The Tragedy of

Julius Caesar

By
WILLIAM SHAKESPEARE

EDITED BY BARBARA A. MOWAT
AND PAUL WERSTINE

AN UPDATED EDITION

SIMON & SCHUSTER PAPERBACKS
NEW YORK LONDON TORONTO SYDNEY NEW DELHI

Simon & Schuster Paperbacks
A Division of Simon & Schuster, Inc.
1230 Avenue of the Americas
New York, NY 10020

Copyright © 1992, 2011 by The Folger Shakespeare Library

This Simon & Schuster paperback edition January 2011

SIMON & SCHUSTER PAPERBACKS and colophon are registered
trademarks of Simon & Schuster, Inc.

For information regarding special discounts for bulk purchases,
please contact Simon & Schuster Special Sales at 1-866-506-1949
or business@simonandschuster.com.

The Simon & Schuster Speakers Bureau can bring authors
to your live event. For more information or to book an
event, contact the Simon & Schuster Speakers Bureau at
1-866-248-3049 or visit our website at www.simonspeakers.com.

Manufactured in the United States of America

30 29 28 27 26 25 24 23

ISBN 978-1-4391-9671-7

From the Director of the Folger Shakespeare Library

It is hard to imagine a world without Shakespeare. Since their composition four hundred years ago, Shakespeare's plays and poems have traveled the globe, inviting those who see and read his works to make them their own.

Readers of the New Folger Editions are part of this on-going process of "taking up Shakespeare," finding our own thoughts and feelings in language that strikes us as old or unusual and, for that very reason, new. We still struggle to keep up with a writer who could think a mile a minute, whose words paint pictures that shift like clouds. These expertly edited texts, presented here with accompanying explanatory notes and up-to-date critical essays, are distinctive because of what they do: they allow readers not simply to keep up, but to engage deeply with a writer whose works invite us to think, and think again.

These New Folger Editions of Shakespeare's plays are also special because of where they come from. The Folger Shakespeare Library in Washington, DC, where the Editions are produced, is the single greatest documentary source of Shakespeare's works. An unparalleled collection of early modern books, manuscripts, and artwork connected to Shakespeare, the Folger's holdings have been consulted extensively in the preparation of these texts. The Editions also reflect the expertise gained through the regular performance of Shakespeare's works in the Folger's Elizabethan Theater.

I want to express my deep thanks to editors Barbara Mowat and Paul Werstine for creating these indispensable editions of Shakespeare's works, which incorporate the best of textual scholarship with a richness of commentary that is both inspired and engaging. Readers who want to know more about Shakespeare and his plays can follow the paths these distinguished scholars have tread by visiting the Folger itself, where a range of physical and digital resources (available online) exist to supplement the material in these texts. I commend to you these words, and hope that they inspire.

Michael Witmore
Director, Folger Shakespeare Library

Contents

Editors' Preface

In recent years, ways of dealing with Shakespeare's texts and with the interpretation of his plays have been undergoing significant change. This edition, while retaining many of the features that have always made the Folger Shakespeare so attractive to the general reader, at the same time reflects these current ways of thinking about Shakespeare. For example, modern readers, actors, and teachers have become interested in the differences between, on the one hand, the early forms in which Shakespeare's plays were first published and, on the other hand, the forms in which editors through the centuries have presented them. In response to this interest, we have based our edition on what we consider the best early printed version of a particular play (explaining our rationale in a section called "An Introduction to This Text") and have marked our changes in the text—unobtrusively, we hope, but in such a way that the curious reader can be aware that a change has been made and can consult the "Textual Notes" to discover what appeared in the early printed version.

Current ways of looking at the plays are reflected in our brief introductions, in many of the commentary notes, in the annotated lists of "Further Reading," and especially in each play's "Modern Perspective," an essay written by an outstanding scholar who brings to the reader his or her fresh assessment of the play in the light of today's interests and concerns.

As in the Folger Library General Reader's Shakespeare, which this edition replaces, we include explanatory notes designed to help make Shakespeare's language clearer to a modern reader, and we place the notes on the page facing the text that they explain. We also follow the earlier edition in including illustrations—of objects, of clothing, of mythological figures—from books and manuscripts in the Folger Shakespeare Library collection. We provide fresh accounts of the life of Shakespeare, of the publishing of his plays, and of the theaters in which his plays were performed, as well as an introduction to the text itself. We also include a section called "Reading Shakespeare's Language," in which we try to help readers learn to "break the code" of Elizabethan poetic language.

For each section of each volume, we are indebted to a host of generous experts and fellow scholars. The "Reading Shakespeare's Language" sections, for example, could not have been written had not Arthur King, of Brigham Young University, and Randal Robinson, author of *Unlocking Shakespeare's Language*, led the way in untangling Shakespearean language puzzles and shared their insights and methodologies generously with us. "Shakespeare's Life" profited by the careful reading given it by S. Schoenbaum; "Shakespeare's Theater" was read and strengthened by Andrew Gurr, John Astington, and William Ingram; and "The Publication of Shakespeare's Plays" is indebted to the comments of Peter W. M. Blayney. We, as editors, take sole responsibility for any errors in our editions.

We are grateful to the authors of the "Modern Perspectives"; to Leeds Barroll and David Bevington for their generous encouragement; to the Huntington and Newberry Libraries for fellowship support; to King's University College for the grants it has provided to Paul Werstine; to the Social Sciences and Humanities Research Council of Canada, which has provided him with Research Time Stipends; to R. J. Shroyer of the University of Western Ontario for essential computer support; and to the Folger Institute's Center for

Shakespeare Studies for its sponsorship of a workshop on "Shakespeare's Texts for Students and Teachers" (funded by the National Endowment for the Humanities and led by Richard Knowles of the University of Wisconsin), a workshop from which we learned an enormous amount about what is wanted by college and high-school teachers of Shakespeare today.

In preparing this preface for the publication of *Julius Caesar* in 1992, we wrote: "Our biggest debt is to the Folger Shakespeare Library: to Werner Gundersheimer, Director of the Library, who has made possible our edition; to Jean Miller, the Library's Art Curator, who combed the Library holdings for illustrations, and to Julie Ainsworth, Head of the Photography Department, who carefully photographed them; to Peggy O'Brien, Director of Education, who gave us expert advice about the needs being expressed by Shakespeare teachers and students (and to Martha Christian and other 'master teachers' who used our texts in manuscript in their classrooms); to the staff of the Academic Programs Division, especially Paul Menzer (who drafted 'Further Reading' material), Mary Tonkinson, Lena Cowen Orlin, Molly Haws, and Jessica Hymowitz; and, finally, to the staff of the Library Reading Room, whose patience and support have been invaluable."

As we revise the play for publication in 2011, we add to the above our gratitude to Gail Kern Paster, Director of the Library since 2002, whose interest and support are unfailing (and whose scholarly expertise is an invaluable resource); to Stephen Llano, our production editor at Simon & Schuster, whose expertise, attention to detail, and wisdom are essential to this project; to Deborah Curren-Aquino, who provides extensive editorial and production support; to Alice Falk for her expert copyediting; to Mary Bloodworth and Michael

Poston for their unfailing computer support; and to the staff of the Library's Research Division, especially Christina Certo (whose help is crucial), David Schalkwyk (Director of Research), Mimi Godfrey, Jennifer Rahm, Kathleen Lynch, Carol Brobeck, Owen Williams, Sarah Werner, and Adrienne Schevchuk. Finally, we once again express our thanks to Jean Miller, who continues to unearth wonderful images, and to the ever-supportive staff of the Library Reading Room.

Barbara A. Mowat and Paul Werstine
2011

Shakespeare's *Julius Caesar*

Shakespeare may have written *Julius Caesar* to be the first of his plays to take the stage at his acting company's new Globe theater in 1599. At this important point in his career as a playwright, Shakespeare turned to a key event in Roman history. Many people in the Renaissance were passionately interested in the story of Caesar's death at the hands of his friends and fellow politicians. There was much debate about who were the villains and who were the heroes. According to the fourteenth-century Italian poet Dante, Brutus and Cassius, the foremost of the conspirators who killed Caesar, were traitors who deserved an eternity in hell. But in the view of Shakespeare's contemporary Sir Philip Sidney, Caesar was a rebel threatening Rome, and Brutus was the wisest of senators.

Shakespeare's dramatization of Caesar's assassination and its aftermath has kept this debate alive among generations of readers and playgoers. Is Brutus the true hero of this tragedy in his principled opposition to Caesar's ambition to become king of Rome? Or is Caesar the tragic hero, the greatest military and civic leader of his era, struck down by lesser men misled by jealousy and false idealism? By continuing to address these questions, our civilization engages not only in the enjoyment of a great play but also in an examination of the ways it chooses to govern itself, whether through the rule of the one (Caesarism, monarchy) or the rule of the many (republicanism).

After you have read the play, we invite you to read "A Modern Perspective" on *Julius Caesar* by Professor Coppélia Kahn of Brown University printed at the back of this book.

The Field of Mars, containing the public buildings of Rome and bounded by the Tiber River on the right. (This picture

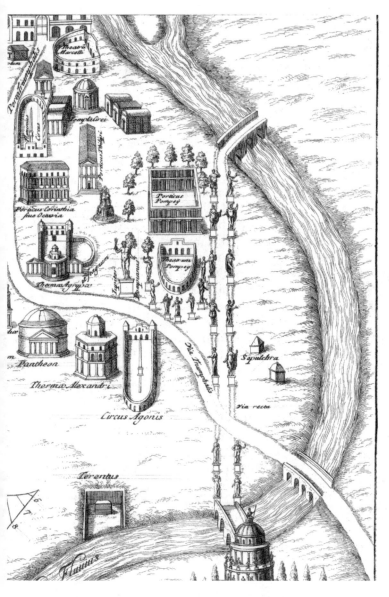

shows the Field at a time later than the time of Julius
Caesar.)   From Alessandro Donati, . . . *Roma* . . . (1694).

Reading Shakespeare's Language: *Julius Caesar*

For many people today, reading Shakespeare's language can be a problem—but it is a problem that can be solved. Those who have studied Latin (or even French or German or Spanish) and those who are used to reading poetry will have little difficulty understanding the language of poetic drama. Others, though, need to develop the skills of untangling unusual sentence structures and of recognizing and understanding poetic compressions, omissions, and wordplay. And even those skilled in reading unusual sentence structures may have occasional trouble with Shakespeare's words. Four hundred years of "static" intervene between his speaking and our hearing. Most of his vocabulary is still in use, but a few of his words are no longer used, and many of his words now have meanings quite different from those they had in the sixteenth century. In the theater, most of these difficulties are solved for us by actors who study the language and articulate it for us so that the essential meaning is heard—or, when combined with stage action, is at least *felt*. When we are reading on our own, we must do what each actor does: go over the lines (often with a dictionary close at hand) until the puzzles are solved and the lines yield up their poetry and the characters speak in words and phrases that are, suddenly, rewarding and wonderfully memorable.

Shakespeare's Words

As you begin to read the opening scenes of a Shakespeare play, you may notice occasional unfamiliar words. Some are unfamiliar simply because we no longer use them. In the opening scenes of *Julius Caesar*, for example, the words *fain* (i.e., gladly), *marry* (an old oath "by the Virgin Mary," which by Shakespeare's time had become a mere interjection, like "indeed"), and *doublet* (a close-fitting jacket worn by Elizabethan men) all appear in Casca's speeches beginning in Act 1, scene 2, line 231 (1.2.231). Words of this kind are explained in notes to the text and will become familiar the more of Shakespeare's plays you read.

In *Julius Caesar*, as in all of Shakespeare's writing, more problematic are the words that are still in use but now have different meanings. In the third line of *Julius Caesar*, for example, the workingmen are called "mechanical"; what is meant is that they are "working men." At 1.2.328, Cassius says that he will throw writings "in several hands" in Brutus's window; we would say "in different handwritings." At 1.2.171, Brutus says "I am nothing jealous" where we might say "I have no doubt." Again, such words are explained in the notes to the text, but they, too, will become familiar as you continue to read Shakespeare's language.

Some words are strange not because of the "static" introduced by changes in language over the past centuries but because they are used by Shakespeare to build a dramatic world that has its own geography and history and story. *Julius Caesar*, for example, builds, in its opening scenes, a location and a past history by frequent references to the Tiber River, to Pompey and to "Pompey's blood" (i.e., Pompey's sons), to the feast of Lupercal, to the Capitol, to "trophies" on the "images," to "soothsayers," to "the ides of March," to Brutus's ancestor (Brutus the Liberator), to the Colossus at Rhodes, and to Aeneas and Anchises. These "local" references (each of which is explained in notes to the text) build the Rome that Brutus, Cassius, and Caesar inhabit and that will become increasingly familiar to you as you get further into the play.

Shakespeare's Sentences

In an English sentence, meaning is quite dependent on the place given each word. "The dog bit the boy" and "The boy bit the dog" mean very different things, even though the individual words are the same. Because English places such importance on the positions of words in sentences, on the way words are arranged, unusual arrangements can puzzle a reader. Shakespeare frequently shifts his sentences away from "normal" English arrangements—often to create the rhythm he seeks, sometimes to use a line's poetic rhythm to emphasize a particular word, sometimes to give a character his or her own speech patterns or to allow the character to speak in a special way. When we attend a good performance of the play, the actors will have worked out the sentence structures and will articulate the sentences so that the meaning is clear. When reading the play, we need to do as the actor does: that is, when puzzled by a character's speech, we check to see if the words are being presented in an unusual sequence.

Look first for the placement of subject and verb. Shakespeare often places the verb before the subject (e.g., instead of "He goes," we find "Goes he"). In the opening scenes of *Julius Caesar*, when Flavius says (1.1.68–69), "Go you down" and "This way will I," he is using such a construction. Caesar does so as well when, at 1.2.220, he says, "therefore are they very dangerous." Shakespeare also frequently places the object before the subject and verb (e.g., instead of "I hit him" we might find "Him I hit"). Brutus's statement to Cassius at 1.2.173–74, "How I have thought of this, and of these times, / I shall recount hereafter," is an example of such an inversion. (The normal order would be "I shall recount . . . how I have thought.") Such constructions are most difficult for us in sentences like that of Cassius at 1.3.95 ("Therein, you gods, you tyrants do defeat"), where "you tyrants" might first be read as the subject of "do defeat"; instead, "you" is the subject and "tyrants" the object. In other words, the normal order here is "you do defeat tyrants."

Inversions are not the only unusual sentence structures in Shakespeare's language. Often his sentences separate words that would normally appear together. (This is usually done to create a particular rhythm or to stress a particular word.) Caesar's "leave no ceremony out" (1.2.14) interrupts the normal phrase "leave out"; Cassius's "as Aeneas, our great ancestor, / Did from the flames of Troy upon his shoulder / The old Anchises bear" (1.2.119–21) separates the two parts of the verb "did bear" with three phrases ("from the flames," "of Troy," "upon his shoulder") and with the verb's object, "The old Anchises." Brutus's "I would not (so with love I might entreat you) / Be any further moved" (1.2.175–76) interrupts the construction "I would not be" by a parenthetical statement that is itself an interrupted construction. To create for yourself sentences that seem more like the English of everyday speech, you may wish to rearrange the words, putting together the word clusters (*"leave out* no ceremony," *"did bear* the old Anchises," *"I would not be* any further moved") and placing the remaining words in their familiar order. The result will usually be an increase in clarity but a loss of rhythm or a shift in emphasis.

Locating and rearranging words that grammatically belong together is especially necessary in passages that separate subjects from verbs and verbs from objects by long delaying or expanding interruptions. When Cassius, at 1.2.327–31, reveals his plan to trick Brutus into thinking the populace is urging Brutus to rise against Caesar, he uses such an interrupted construction, as if to disguise from himself or from us the simple sense of what he is saying. To understand him, one needs to figure out that the basic elements of the sentence are "I will throw writings in at his windows." Cassius's version reads, "*I will* this night / In several hands [i.e., handwritings] in at his windows *throw*, / As if they came from several citizens, / *Writings*, all tending to the great opinion / That Rome holds of his name. . . ." A less complicated example of this same interrupted construction is used by Cassius again at 1.3.126–29: "Now know you, Casca, I have moved already / Some certain of the noblest-minded Romans / To undergo with me an enterprise / Of honorable-dangerous consequence," where the basic sentence-elements are simply "I have moved certain Romans to undergo an enterprise."

Shakespeare's sentences are sometimes complicated not because of unusual structures or interruptions but because he omits words and parts of words that English sentences normally require. (In conversation, we, too, often omit words. We say, "Heard from him yet?" and our hearer supplies the missing "Have you.") In plays written ten years or so after *Julius Caesar*, Shakespeare uses omissions both of verbs and of nouns to great dramatic effect. In *Julius Caesar* omissions are few and seem to be the effect of compressed expression. At 1.1.30, for instance, Flavius asks, "But wherefore [i.e., why] art not in thy shop today?" omitting the subject, "thou," and creating a rhythmically regular line. At 1.1.74, he omits the verb "go" and says simply, "I'll about." At 1.2.82, Cassius drops the second syllable of "afterward" in saying, "And after scandal [i.e., slander] them." At 1.2.117, he omits the preposition "at" in saying "But ere we could arrive [at] the point proposed," and at 1.2.191 he omits the preposition "of" in the phrase "worthy [of] note." At 1.2.324 he asks "who so firm" rather than "who is so firm," and at 1.3.130 he omits a noun in the line "I do know, by this [time? hour?] they stay for me."

Finally, one finds in all of Shakespeare's plays constructions that do not fit any particular category, each of which must be untangled on its own. In *Julius Caesar* Flavius says, at 1.1.66, "See whe'er [whether] their basest mettle be not moved," where the context makes clear that he means "Look, the lowest one of them is emotionally touched." (This construction—"whether" followed by a negative verb—occurs also in *Hamlet*, where again it yields a positive statement.) At 1.2.11, the phrase "sterile curse" means "curse of sterility." (In *The Merchant of Venice* [1.1.85], one finds a comparable construction in "old wrinkles," meaning "the wrinkles of old age.") Such constructions are explained in the notes to the text and must simply be handled as individual puzzles to be solved.

Shakespearean Wordplay

Shakespeare plays with language so often and so variously that entire books are written on the topic. Here we will mention only two kinds of wordplay, puns and metaphors. A pun is a play on words that sound the same but have different meanings (or on a single word

that has more than one meaning). When, in the opening scene of *Julius Caesar*, one of the "mechanicals"
answers Marullus's question about his trade by saying
that he is "a cobbler," he leads Marullus and Flavius to
think that he is using the word to mean "a bungler."
Only several lines of dialogue later do they realize that
he is, in fact, a shoemaker (the other meaning of that
word). Within that dialogue, the cobbler also puns
on "withal" (which means "nevertheless," but which
sounds also like "with awl"). If one is not aware that
a character is punning, the dialogue can seem simply
silly or unintelligible. One must stay alert, then, to
the sounds of words and to the possibility of double
meanings.

A metaphor is a play on words in which one object
or idea is expressed as if it were something else, something with which the metaphor suggests it shares
common features. For instance, when Brutus says, at
4.3.249, "There is a tide in the affairs of men," and goes
on to talk about the voyage of a man's life, he is using
metaphoric language. As a good sailor embarks when
the tide is high, so a clever man senses when his pros-
pects are favorable and takes advantage of the "full sea."
When Cassius, at 1.2.40–41, says to Brutus, "You bear
too stubborn and too strange a hand / Over your friend
that loves you," Cassius is using metaphoric language,
likening Brutus to a horseback rider who handles the
reins of the horse harshly. And at 2.1.69–72, when Brutus wants to describe the turmoil within himself as he
contemplates the possibility of killing Caesar, he uses
metaphoric language in which his being is likened to
a state suffering an insurrection. Metaphors are often
used when the idea being conveyed is hard to express,
and the speaker is thus given language that helps to
carry the idea or the feeling to his or her listener—and
to the audience.

Implied Stage Action

Finally, in reading Shakespeare's plays we should always remember that what we are reading is a performance script. The dialogue is written to be spoken by actors who, at the same time, are moving, gesturing, picking up objects, weeping, shaking their fists. Some stage action is described in what are called "stage directions"; some is signaled within the dialogue itself. We must learn to be alert to such signals as we stage the play in our imaginations. When, at 1.2.24 in *Julius Caesar*, Caesar says, "Set him before me. Let me see his face," and Cassius says, "Fellow, come from the throng. Look upon Caesar" (1.2.25–26), it can be assumed that the Soothsayer moves through the crowd of actors to stand before Caesar, so that Caesar can then say, "What sayst thou to me now?" (When stage actions are so clearly demanded by the dialogue, this edition will normally add a stage direction.) Again, at 1.2.225, when Casca says, "You pulled me by the cloak," it is clear what has happened—though the director (and we, in our imaginations) can choose whether Brutus or Cassius performed the action. Learning to read the language of stage action repays one many times over when one reaches a crucial scene like that of the assassination (3.1), where the carefully choreographed kneelings and stabbings are indicated almost completely in the dialogue (though this edition adds some stage directions), and where one must simultaneously understand metaphoric language and the gesture it implies (so that one understands that the line "Metellus Cimber throws before thy seat / An humble heart" [3.1.37–38] indicates that the actor here kneels at Caesar's feet, and that Casca's "Speak, hands, for me!" [3.1.84] indicates that Casca here stabs Caesar).

It is immensely rewarding to work carefully with Shakespeare's language—the words, the sentences, the wordplay, and the implied stage actions—as readers for the past four centuries have discovered. It may be more pleasurable to attend a good performance of a play—though not everyone has thought so. But the joy of being able to stage a Shakespeare play in our imaginations, to return to passages that continue to yield further meanings (or further questions) the more one reads them—these are pleasures that, for many, rival (or at least augment) those of the performed text, and certainly make it worth considerable effort to "break the code" of Elizabethan poetic drama and let free the remarkable language that makes up a Shakespeare text.

Shakespeare's Life

Surviving documents that give us glimpses into the life of William Shakespeare show us a playwright, poet, and actor who grew up in the market town of Stratford-upon-Avon, spent his professional life in London, and returned to Stratford a wealthy landowner. He was born in April 1564, died in April 1616, and is buried inside the chancel of Holy Trinity Church in Stratford.

We wish we could know more about the life of the world's greatest dramatist. His plays and poems are testaments to his wide reading—especially to his knowledge of Virgil, Ovid, Plutarch, Holinshed's *Chronicles*, and the Bible—and to his mastery of the English language, but we can only speculate about his education. We know that the King's New School in Stratford-upon-Avon was considered excellent. The school was one of the English "grammar schools" established to educate young men, primarily in Latin grammar and literature. As in other schools of the time, students began their studies at the age of four or five in the attached "petty school," and there learned to read and write in English, studying primarily the catechism from the Book of Common Prayer. After two years in the petty school, students entered the lower form (grade) of the grammar school, where they began the serious study of Latin grammar and Latin texts that would occupy most of the remainder of their school days. (Several Latin texts that Shakespeare used repeatedly in writing his plays and poems were texts that schoolboys memorized and recited.) Latin comedies were introduced early in the lower form; in the upper form, which the boys entered at age ten or eleven, students wrote their own Latin orations and declamations, studied Latin

Title page of a 1573 Latin and Greek catechism for children.
From Alexander Nowell, *Catechismus paruus pueris
primum Latine* . . . (1573).

historians and rhetoricians, and began the study of Greek using the Greek New Testament.

Since the records of the Stratford "grammar school" do not survive, we cannot prove that William Shakespeare attended the school; however, every indication (his father's position as an alderman and bailiff of Stratford, the playwright's own knowledge of the Latin classics, scenes in the plays that recall grammar-school experiences—for example, *The Merry Wives of Windsor*, 4.1) suggests that he did. We also lack generally accepted documentation about Shakespeare's life after his schooling ended and his professional life in London began. His marriage in 1582 (at age eighteen) to Anne Hathaway and the subsequent births of his daughter Susanna (1583) and the twins Judith and Hamnet (1585) are recorded, but how he supported himself and where he lived are not known. Nor do we know when and why he left Stratford for the London theatrical world, nor how he rose to be the important figure in that world that he had become by the early 1590s.

We do know that by 1592 he had achieved some prominence in London as both an actor and a playwright. In that year was published a book by the playwright Robert Greene attacking an actor who had the audacity to write blank-verse drama and who was "in his own conceit [i.e., opinion] the only Shake-scene in a country." Since Greene's attack includes a parody of a line from one of Shakespeare's early plays, there is little doubt that it is Shakespeare to whom he refers, a "Shake-scene" who had aroused Greene's fury by successfully competing with university-educated dramatists like Greene himself. It was in 1593 that Shakespeare became a published poet. In that year he published his long narrative poem *Venus and Adonis*; in 1594, he followed it with *The Rape of Lucrece*. Both poems were dedicated to the young earl of Southampton (Henry Wriothesley), who may have become Shakespeare's patron.

It seems no coincidence that Shakespeare wrote these narrative poems at a time when the theaters were closed because of the plague, a contagious epidemic disease that devastated the population of London. When the theaters reopened in 1594, Shakespeare apparently resumed his double career of actor and playwright and began his long (and seemingly profitable) service as an acting-company shareholder. Records for December of 1594 show him to be a leading member of the Lord Chamberlain's Men. It was this company of actors, later named the King's Men, for whom he would be a principal actor, dramatist, and shareholder for the rest of his career.

So far as we can tell, that career spanned about twenty years. In the 1590s, he wrote his plays on English history as well as several comedies and at least two tragedies (*Titus Andronicus* and *Romeo and Juliet*). These histories, comedies, and tragedies are the plays credited to him in 1598 in a work, *Palladis Tamia*, that in one chapter compares English writers with "Greek, Latin, and Italian Poets." There the author, Francis Meres, claims that Shakespeare is comparable to the Latin dramatists Seneca for tragedy and Plautus for comedy, and calls him "the most excellent in both kinds for the stage." He also names him "Mellifluous and honey-tongued Shakespeare": "I say," writes Meres, "that the Muses would speak with Shakespeare's fine filed phrase, if they would speak English." Since Meres also mentions Shakespeare's "sugared sonnets among his private friends," it is assumed that many of Shakespeare's sonnets (not published until 1609) were also written in the 1590s.

In 1599, Shakespeare's company built a theater for themselves across the river from London, naming it the Globe. The plays that are considered by many to be Shakespeare's major tragedies (*Hamlet, Othello, King Lear,* and *Macbeth*) were written while the company was resident in this theater, as were such comedies as *Twelfth Night* and *Measure for Measure.* Many of Shakespeare's plays were performed at court (both for Queen Elizabeth I and, after her death in 1603, for King James I), some were presented at the Inns of Court (the residences of London's legal societies), and some were doubtless performed in other towns, at the universities, and at great houses when the King's Men went on tour; otherwise, his plays from 1599 to 1608 were, so far as we know, performed only at the Globe. Between 1608 and 1612, Shakespeare wrote several plays—among them *The Winter's Tale* and *The Tempest*—presumably for the company's new indoor Blackfriars theater, though the plays seem to have been performed also at the Globe and at court. Surviving documents describe a performance of *The Winter's Tale* in 1611 at the Globe, for example, and performances of *The Tempest* in 1611 and 1613 at the royal palace of Whitehall.

Shakespeare wrote very little after 1612, the year in which he probably wrote *King Henry VIII.* (It was at a performance of *Henry VIII* in 1613 that the Globe caught fire and burned to the ground.) Sometime between 1610 and 1613 he seems to have returned to live in Stratford-upon-Avon, where he owned a large house and considerable property, and where his wife and his two daughters and their husbands lived. (His son Hamnet had died in 1596.) During his professional years in London, Shakespeare had presumably derived income from the acting company's profits as well as from his own career as an actor, from the sale of his play manuscripts to the acting company, and, after 1599, from his shares as an owner of the Globe. It was presumably that income, carefully invested in land

Ptolemaic universe.
From Marcus Manilius, *The sphere of . . .* (1675).

and other property, that made him the wealthy man that surviving documents show him to have become. It is also assumed that William Shakespeare's growing wealth and reputation played some part in inclining the Crown, in 1596, to grant John Shakespeare, William's father, the coat of arms that he had so long sought. William Shakespeare died in Stratford on April 23, 1616 (according to the epitaph carved under his bust in Holy Trinity Church) and was buried on April 25. Seven years after his death, his collected plays were published as *Mr. William Shakespeares Comedies, Histories, & Tragedies* (the work now known as the First Folio).

The years in which Shakespeare wrote were among the most exciting in English history. Intellectually, the discovery, translation, and printing of Greek and Roman classics were making available a set of works and worldviews that interacted complexly with Christian texts and beliefs. The result was a questioning, a vital intellectual ferment, that provided energy for the period's amazing dramatic and literary output and that fed directly into Shakespeare's plays. The Ghost in *Hamlet*, for example, is wonderfully complicated in part because he is a figure from Roman tragedy—the spirit of the dead returning to seek revenge—who at the same time inhabits a Christian hell (or purgatory); Hamlet's description of humankind reflects at one moment the Neoplatonic wonderment at mankind ("What a piece of work is a man!") and, at the next, the Christian disparagement of human sinners ("And yet, to me, what is this quintessence of dust?").

As intellectual horizons expanded, so also did geographical and cosmological horizons. New worlds—both North and South America—were explored, and in them were found human beings who lived and worshiped in ways radically different from those of Renaissance Europeans and Englishmen. The universe during these years also seemed to shift and expand. Copernicus had earlier theorized that the earth was not the center of the cosmos but revolved as a planet around the sun. Galileo's telescope, created in 1609, allowed scientists to see that Copernicus had been correct: the universe was not organized with the earth at the center, nor was it so nicely circumscribed as people had, until that time, thought. In terms of expanding horizons, the impact of these discoveries on people's beliefs—religious, scientific, and philosophical—cannot be overstated.

London, too, rapidly expanded and changed during the years (from the early 1590s to around 1610) that Shakespeare lived there. London—the center of England's government, its economy, its royal court, its overseas trade—was, during these years, becoming an exciting metropolis, drawing to it thousands of new citizens every year. Troubled by overcrowding, by poverty, by recurring epidemics of the plague, London was also a mecca for the wealthy and the aristocratic, and for those who sought advancement at court, or power in government or finance or trade. One hears in Shakespeare's plays the voices of London—the struggles for power, the fear of venereal disease, the language of buying and selling. One hears as well the voices of Stratford-upon-Avon—references to the nearby Forest of Arden, to sheepherding, to small-town gossip, to village fairs and markets. Part of the richness of Shakespeare's work is the influence felt there of the various worlds in which he lived: the world of metropolitan London, the world of small-town and rural England, the world of the theater, and the worlds of craftsmen and shepherds.

That Shakespeare inhabited such worlds we know from surviving London and Stratford documents, as well as from the evidence of the plays and poems themselves. From such records we can sketch the dramatist's life. We know from his works that he was a voracious reader. We know from legal and business documents that he was a multifaceted theater man who became a wealthy landowner. We know a bit about his family life and a fair amount about his legal and financial dealings. Most scholars today depend upon such evidence as they draw their picture of the world's greatest playwright. Such, however, has not always been the case. Until the late eighteenth century, the William Shakespeare who lived in most biographies was the creation of legend and tradition. This was the Shakespeare who was supposedly caught poaching deer at Charlecote, the estate of Sir Thomas Lucy close by Stratford; this was the Shakespeare who fled from Sir Thomas's vengeance and made his way in London by taking care of horses outside a playhouse; this was the Shakespeare who reportedly could barely read, but whose natural gifts were extraordinary, whose father was a butcher who allowed his gifted son sometimes to help in the butcher shop, where William supposedly killed calves "in a high style," making a speech for the occasion. It was this legendary William Shakespeare whose Falstaff (in *1* and *2 Henry IV*) so pleased Queen Elizabeth that she demanded a play about Falstaff in love, and demanded that it be written in fourteen days (hence the existence of *The Merry Wives of Windsor*). It was this legendary Shakespeare who reached the top of his acting career in the roles of the Ghost in *Hamlet* and old Adam in *As You Like It*—and who died of a fever contracted by drinking too hard at "a merry meeting" with the poets Michael Drayton and Ben Jonson. This legendary Shakespeare is a rambunctious, undisciplined man, as attractively "wild" as his plays were seen by earlier generations to be. Unfortunately, there is no trace of evidence to support these wonderful stories.

Perhaps in response to the disreputable Shakespeare of legend—or perhaps in response to the fragmentary and, for some, all-too-ordinary Shakespeare documented by surviving records—some people since the mid–nineteenth century have argued that William Shakespeare could not have written the plays that bear his name. These persons have put forward some dozen names as more likely authors, among them Queen Elizabeth, Sir Francis Bacon, Edward de Vere (earl of Oxford), and Christopher Marlowe. Such attempts to find what for these people is a more believable author of the plays is a tribute to the regard in which the plays are held. Unfortunately for their claims, the documents that exist that provide evidence for the facts of Shakespeare's life tie him inextricably to the body of plays and poems that bear his name. Unlikely as it seems to those who want the works to have been written by an aristocrat, a university graduate, or an "important" person, the plays and poems seem clearly to have been produced by a man from Stratford-upon-Avon with a very good "grammar-school" education and a life of experience in London and in the world of the London theater. How this particular man produced the works that dominate the cultures of much of the world almost four hundred years after his death is one of life's mysteries—and one that will continue to tease our imaginations as we continue to delight in his plays and poems.

Shakespeare's Theater

The actors of Shakespeare's time are known to have performed plays in a great variety of locations. They played at court (that is, in the great halls of such royal residences as Whitehall, Hampton Court, and Greenwich); they played in halls at the universities of Oxford and Cambridge, and at the Inns of Court (the residences in London of the legal societies); and they also played in the private houses of great lords and civic officials. Sometimes acting companies went on tour from London into the provinces, often (but not only) when outbreaks of bubonic plague in the capital forced the closing of theaters to reduce the possibility of contagion in crowded audiences. In the provinces the actors usually staged their plays in churches (until around 1600) or in guildhalls. While surviving records show only a handful of occasions when actors played at inns while on tour, London inns were important playing places up until the 1590s.

The building of theaters in London had begun only shortly before Shakespeare wrote his first plays in the 1590s. These theaters were of two kinds: outdoor or public playhouses that could accommodate large numbers of playgoers, and indoor or private theaters for much smaller audiences. What is usually regarded as the first London outdoor public playhouse was called simply the Theatre. James Burbage—the father of Richard Burbage, who was perhaps the most famous actor in Shakespeare's company—built it in 1576 in an area north of the city of London called Shoreditch. Among the more famous of the other public playhouses that capitalized on the new fashion were the Curtain and the Fortune (both also built north of the city), the Rose,

A stylized representation of the Globe theater.
From Claes Jansz Visscher, *Londinum florentissima Britanniae urbs* . . . [c. 1625].

the Swan, the Globe, and the Hope (all located on the Bankside, a region just across the Thames south of the city of London). All these playhouses had to be built outside the jurisdiction of the city of London because many civic officials were hostile to the performance of drama and repeatedly petitioned the royal council to abolish it.

The theaters erected on the Bankside (a region under the authority of the Church of England, whose head was the monarch) shared the neighborhood with houses of prostitution and with the Paris Garden, where the blood sports of bearbaiting and bullbaiting were carried on. There may have been no clear distinction between playhouses and buildings for such sports, for we know that the Hope was used for both plays and baiting and that Philip Henslowe, owner of the Rose and, later, partner in the ownership of the Fortune, was also a partner in a monopoly on baiting. All these forms of entertainment were easily accessible to Londoners by boat across the Thames or over London Bridge.

Evidently Shakespeare's company prospered on the Bankside. They moved there in 1599. Threatened by difficulties in renewing the lease on the land where their first theater (the Theatre) had been built, Shakespeare's company took advantage of the Christmas holiday in 1598 to dismantle the Theatre and transport its timbers across the Thames to the Bankside, where, in 1599, these timbers were used in the building of the Globe. The weather in late December 1598 is recorded as having been especially harsh. It was so cold that the Thames was "nigh [nearly] frozen," and there was heavy snow. Perhaps the weather aided Shakespeare's company in eluding their landlord, the snow hiding their activity and the freezing of the Thames allowing them to slide the timbers across to the Bankside without paying tolls for repeated trips over London Bridge.

Attractive as this narrative is, it remains just as likely that the heavy snow hampered transport of the timbers in wagons through the London streets to the river. It also must be remembered that the Thames was, according to report, only "nigh frozen," and therefore not necessarily providing solid footing. Whatever the precise circumstances of this fascinating event in English theater history, Shakespeare's company was able to begin playing at their new Globe theater on the Bankside in 1599. After this theater burned down in 1613 during the staging of Shakespeare's *Henry VIII* (its thatch roof was set alight by cannon fire called for in performance), Shakespeare's company immediately rebuilt on the same location. The second Globe seems to have been a grander structure than its predecessor. It remained in use until the beginning of the English Civil War in 1642, when Parliament officially closed the theaters. Soon thereafter it was pulled down.

The public theaters of Shakespeare's time were very different buildings from our theaters today. First of all, they were open-air playhouses. As recent excavations of the Rose and the Globe confirm, some were polygonal or roughly circular in shape; the Fortune, however, was square. The most recent estimates of their size put the diameter of these buildings at 72 feet (the Rose) to 100 feet (the Globe), but we know that they held vast audiences of two or three thousand, who must have been squeezed together quite tightly. Some of these spectators paid extra to sit or stand in the two or three levels of roofed galleries that extended, on the upper levels, all the way around the theater and surrounded an open space. In this space were the stage and, perhaps, the tiring house (what we would call dressing rooms), as well as the so-called yard. In the yard stood the spectators who chose to pay less, the ones whom Hamlet contemptuously called "groundlings." For a roof they had only the sky, and so they were exposed to all kinds of weather. They stood on a floor that was sometimes made of mortar and sometimes of ash mixed with the shells of hazelnuts, which, it has recently been discovered, were standard flooring material in the period.

Unlike the yard, the stage itself was covered by a roof. Its ceiling, called "the heavens," is thought to have been elaborately painted to depict the sun, moon, stars, and planets. The exact size of the stage remains hard to determine. We have a single sketch of part of the interior of the Swan. A Dutchman named Johannes de Witt visited this theater around 1596 and sent a sketch of it back to his friend, Arend van Buchel. Because van Buchel found de Witt's letter and sketch of interest, he copied both into a book. It is van Buchel's copy, adapted, it seems, to the shape and size of the page in his book, that survives. In this sketch, the stage appears to be a large rectangular platform that thrusts far out into the yard, perhaps even as far as the center of the circle formed by the surrounding galleries. This drawing, combined with the specifications for the size of the stage in the building contract for the Fortune, has led scholars to conjecture that the stage on which Shakespeare's plays were performed must have measured approximately 43 feet in width and 27 feet in depth, a vast acting area. But the digging up of a large part of the Rose by late-twentieth-century archaeologists has provided evidence of a quite different stage design. The Rose stage was a platform tapered at the corners and much shallower than what seems to be depicted in the van Buchel sketch. Indeed, its measurements seem to be about 37.5 feet across at its widest point and only 15.5 feet deep. Because the surviving indications of stage size and design differ from each other so much, it is possible that the stages in other theaters, like the Theatre, the Curtain, and the Globe (the outdoor playhouses where we know that Shakespeare's plays were performed), were different from those at both the Swan and the Rose.

After about 1608 Shakespeare's plays were staged not only at the Globe but also at an indoor or private playhouse in Blackfriars. This theater had been constructed in 1596 by James Burbage in an upper hall of a former Dominican priory or monastic house. Although Henry VIII had dissolved all English monasteries in the 1530s (shortly after he had founded the Church of England), the area remained under church, rather than hostile civic, control. The hall that Burbage had purchased and renovated was a large one in which Parliament had once met. In the private theater that he constructed, the stage, lit by candles, was built across the narrow end of the hall, with boxes flanking it. The rest of the hall offered seating room only. Because there was no provision for standing room, the largest audience it could hold was less than a thousand, or about a quarter of what the Globe could accommodate. Admission to Blackfriars was correspondingly more expensive. Instead of a penny to stand in the yard at the Globe, it cost a minimum of sixpence to get into Blackfriars. The best seats at the Globe (in the Lords' Room in the gallery above and behind the stage) cost sixpence; but the boxes flanking the stage at Blackfriars were half a crown, or five times sixpence. Some spectators who were particularly interested in displaying themselves paid even more to sit on stools on the Blackfriars stage.

Whether in the outdoor or indoor playhouses, the stages of Shakespeare's time were different from ours. They were not separated from the audience by the dropping of a curtain between acts and scenes. Therefore the playwrights of the time had to find other ways of signaling to the audience that one scene (to be imagined as occurring in one location at a given time) had ended and the next (to be imagined at perhaps a different location at a later time) had begun. The customary way used by Shakespeare and many of his contemporaries was to have everyone on stage exit at the end of one scene and have one or more different characters enter to begin the next. In a few cases, where characters remain onstage from one scene to another, the dialogue or stage action makes the change of location clear, and the characters are generally to be imagined as having moved from one place to another. For example, in *Romeo and Juliet*, Romeo and his friends remain onstage in Act 1 from scene 4 to scene 5, but they are represented as having moved between scenes from the street that leads to Capulet's house into Capulet's house itself. The new location is signaled in part by the appearance onstage of Capulet's servingmen carrying napkins, something they would not take into the streets. Playwrights had to be quite resourceful in the use of hand properties, like the napkin, or in the use of dialogue to specify where the action was taking place in their plays because, in contrast to most of today's theaters, the playhouses of Shakespeare's time did not fill the stage with scenery to make the setting precise. A consequence of this difference was that the playwrights of Shakespeare's time did not have to specify exactly where the action of their plays was set when they did not choose to do so, and much of the action of their plays is tied to no specific place.

Usually Shakespeare's stage is referred to as a "bare stage," to distinguish it from the stages of the last two or three centuries with their elaborate sets. But the stage in Shakespeare's time was not completely bare. Philip Henslowe, owner of the Rose, lists in his inventory of stage properties a rock, three tombs, and two mossy banks. Stage directions in plays of the time also call for such things as thrones (or "states"), banquets (presumably tables with plaster replicas of food on them), and beds and tombs to be pushed onto the stage. Thus the stage often held more than the actors.

The actors did not limit their performing to the stage alone. Occasionally they went beneath the stage, as the Ghost appears to do in the first act of *Hamlet*. From there they could emerge onto the stage through a trapdoor. They could retire behind the hangings across the back of the stage, as, for example, the actor playing Polonius does when he hides behind the arras. Sometimes the hangings could be drawn back during a performance to "discover" one or more actors behind them. When performance required that an actor appear "above," as when Juliet is imagined to stand at the window of her chamber in the famous and misnamed "balcony scene," then the actor probably climbed the stairs to the gallery over the back of the stage and temporarily shared it with some of the spectators. The stage was also provided with ropes and winches so that actors could descend from, and reascend to, the "heavens."

Perhaps the greatest difference between dramatic performances in Shakespeare's time and ours was that in Shakespeare's England the roles of women were played by boys. (Some of these boys grew up to take male roles in their maturity.) There were no women in the acting companies. It had not always been so in the history of the English stage. There are records of women on English stages in the thirteenth and fourteenth centuries, two hundred years before Shakespeare's plays were performed. After the accession of James I in 1603, the queen of England and her ladies took part in entertainments at court called masques, and with the reopening of the theaters in 1660 at the restoration of Charles II, women again took their place on the public stage.

The chief competitors of such acting companies as the one to which Shakespeare belonged and for which he wrote were companies of exclusively boy actors. The competition was most intense in the early 1600s. There were then two principal children's companies: the Children of Paul's (the choirboys from St. Paul's Cathedral, whose private playhouse was near the cathedral); and the Children of the Chapel Royal (the choirboys from the monarch's private chapel, who performed at the Blackfriars theater built by Burbage in 1596). In *Hamlet* Shakespeare writes of "an aerie [nest] of children, little eyases [hawks], that cry out on the top of question and are most tyrannically clapped for 't. These are now the fashion and . . . berattle the common stages [attack the public theaters]." In the long run, the adult actors prevailed. The Children of Paul's dissolved around 1606. By about 1608 the Children of the Chapel Royal had been forced to stop playing at the Blackfriars theater, which was then taken over by the King's Men, Shakespeare's own troupe.

Acting companies and theaters of Shakespeare's time seem to have been organized in various ways. For example, with the building of the Globe, Shakespeare's company apparently managed itself, with the principal actors, Shakespeare among them, having the status of "sharers" and the right to a share in the takings, as well as the responsibility for a part of the expenses. Five of the sharers, including Shakespeare, owned the Globe. As actor, as sharer in an acting company and in ownership of theaters, and as playwright, Shakespeare was about as involved in the theatrical industry as one could imagine. Although Shakespeare and his fellows prospered, their status under the law was conditional upon the protection of powerful patrons. "Common players"—those who did not have patrons or masters—were classed in the language of the law with "vagabonds and sturdy beggars." So the actors had to secure for themselves the official rank of servants of patrons. Among the patrons under whose protection Shakespeare's company worked were the lord chamberlain and, after the accession of King James in 1603, the king himself.

In the early 1990s we seemed on the verge of learning a great deal more about the theaters in which Shakespeare and his contemporaries performed—or, at least, opening up new questions about them. At that time about 70 percent of the Rose had been excavated, as had about 10 percent of the second Globe, the one built in 1614. It was then hoped that more would become available for study. However, excavation was halted at that point, and while it is not known if or when it will resume at these sites, archaeological discoveries in Shoreditch in 2008 in the vicinity of the Theatre may yield new information about the playhouses of Shakespeare's London.

The Publication of Shakespeare's Plays

Eighteen of Shakespeare's plays found their way into print during the playwright's lifetime, but there is nothing to suggest that he took any interest in their publication. These eighteen appeared separately in editions in quarto or, in the case of *Henry VI, Part 3*, octavo format. The quarto pages are not much larger than a modern mass-market paperback book, and the octavo pages are even smaller; these little books were sold unbound for a few pence. The earliest of the quartos that still survive were printed in 1594, the year that both *Titus Andronicus* and a version of the play now called *Henry VI, Part 2* became available. While almost every one of these early quartos displays on its title page the name of the acting company that performed the play, only about half provide the name of the playwright, Shakespeare. The first quarto edition to bear the name Shakespeare on its title page is *Love's Labor's Lost* of 1598. A few of the quartos were popular with the book-buying public of Shakespeare's lifetime; for example, quarto *Richard II* went through five editions between 1597 and 1615. But most of the quartos were far from best sellers; *Love's Labor's Lost* (1598), for instance, was not reprinted in quarto until 1631. After Shakespeare's death, two more of his plays appeared in quarto format: *Othello* in 1622 and *The Two Noble Kinsmen*, coauthored with John Fletcher, in 1634.

In 1623, seven years after Shakespeare's death, *Mr. William Shakespeares Comedies, Histories, & Tragedies* was published. This printing offered readers in a single book thirty-six of the thirty-eight plays now thought to have been written by Shakespeare, including eighteen that had never been printed before. And it offered them in a style that was then reserved for serious literature and scholarship. The plays were arranged in double columns on pages nearly a foot high. This large page size is called "folio," as opposed to the smaller "quarto," and the 1623 volume is usually called the Shakespeare First Folio. It is reputed to have sold for the lordly price of a pound. (One copy at the Folger Shakespeare Library is marked fifteen shillings—that is, three-quarters of a pound.)

In a preface to the First Folio entitled "To the great Variety of Readers," two of Shakespeare's former fellow actors in the King's Men, John Heminge and Henry Condell, wrote that they themselves had collected their dead companion's plays. They suggested that they had seen his own papers: "we have scarce received from him a blot in his papers." The title page of the Folio declared that the plays within it had been printed "according to the True Original Copies." Comparing the Folio to the quartos, Heminge and Condell disparaged the quartos, advising their readers that "before you were abused with divers stolen and surreptitious copies, maimed, and deformed by the frauds and stealths of injurious impostors." Many Shakespeareans of the eighteenth and nineteenth centuries believed Heminge and Condell and regarded the Folio plays as superior to anything in the quartos.

Once we begin to examine the Folio plays in detail, it becomes less easy to take at face value the word of Heminge and Condell about the superiority of the Folio texts. For example, of the first nine plays in the Folio (one-quarter of the entire collection), four were essentially reprinted from earlier quarto printings that Heminge and Condell had disparaged, and four have now been identified as printed from copies written in the hand of a professional scribe of the 1620s named Ralph Crane; the ninth, *The Comedy of Errors*, was apparently also printed from a manuscript, but one whose origin cannot be readily identified. Evidently, then, eight of the first nine plays in the First Folio were not printed, in spite of what the Folio title page announces, "according to the True Original Copies," or Shakespeare's own papers, and the source of the ninth is unknown. Since today's editors have been forced to treat Heminge and Condell's pronouncements with skepticism, they must choose whether to base their own editions upon quartos or the Folio on grounds other than Heminge and Condell's story of where the quarto and Folio versions originated.

Editors have often fashioned their own narratives to explain what lies behind the quartos and Folio. They have said that Heminge and Condell meant to criticize only a few of the early quartos, the ones that offer much shorter and sometimes quite different, often garbled, versions of plays. Among the examples of these are the 1600 quarto of *Henry V* (the Folio offers a much fuller version) or the 1603 *Hamlet* quarto. (In 1604 a different, much longer form of the play got into print as a quarto.) Early twentieth-century editors speculated that these questionable texts were produced when someone in the audience took notes from the plays' dialogue during performances and then employed "hack poets" to fill out the notes. The poor results were then sold to a publisher and presented in print as Shakespeare's plays. More recently this story has given way to another in which the shorter versions are said to be re-creations from memory of Shakespeare's plays by actors who wanted to stage them in the provinces but lacked manuscript copies. Most of the quartos offer much better texts than these so-called bad quartos. Indeed, in most of the quartos we find texts that are at least equal to or better than what is printed in the Folio. Many Shakespeare enthusiasts persuaded themselves that most of the quartos were set into type directly from Shakespeare's own papers, although there is nothing on which to base this conclusion except the desire for it to be true. Thus speculation continues about how the Shakespeare plays got to be printed. All that we have are the printed texts.

The book collector who was most successful in bringing together copies of the quartos and the First Folio was Henry Clay Folger, founder of the Folger Shakespeare Library in Washington, D.C. While it is estimated that there survive around the world only about 230 copies of the First Folio, Mr. Folger was able to acquire more than seventy-five copies, as well as a large number of fragments, for the library that bears his name. He also amassed a substantial number of quartos. For example, only fourteen copies of the First Quarto of *Love's Labor's Lost* are known to exist, and three are at the Folger Shakespeare Library. As a consequence of Mr. Folger's labors, scholars visiting the Folger Shakespeare Library have been able to learn a great deal about sixteenth- and seventeenth-century printing and, particularly, about the printing of Shakespeare's plays. And Mr. Folger did not stop at the First Folio, but collected many copies of later editions of Shakespeare, beginning with the Second Folio (1632), the Third (1663–64), and the Fourth (1685). Each of these later folios was based on its immediate predecessor and was edited anonymously. The first editor of Shakespeare whose name we know was Nicholas Rowe, whose first edition came out in 1709. Mr. Folger collected this edition and many, many more by Rowe's successors, and the collecting continues.

An Introduction to This Text

Julius Caesar was first printed in the 1623 collection of Shakespeare's plays now known as the First Folio. The present edition is based directly upon that printing.* For the convenience of the reader, we have modernized the punctuation and the spelling of the Folio text. Sometimes we go so far as to modernize certain old forms of words; for example, usually when *a* means "he," we change it to *he*; we change *mo* to *more*, *ye* to *you*, and *god buy to you* to *good-bye to you*. It is not our practice in editing any of the plays to modernize words that sound distinctly different from modern forms. For example, when the early printed texts read *sith* or *apricocks* or *porpentine*, we have not modernized to *since, apricots, porcupine*. When the forms *an, and*, or *and if* appear instead of the modern form *if*, we have reduced *and* to *an* but have not changed any of these forms to their modern equivalent, *if*. We also modernize and, where necessary, correct passages in foreign languages, unless an error in the early printed text can be reasonably explained as a joke.

Whenever we change the wording of the First Folio or add anything to its stage directions, we mark the change by enclosing it in superior half-brackets (⌐ ¬). We want our readers to be immediately aware when we have intervened. (Only when we correct an obvious typographical error in the First Folio does the change not get marked.) Whenever we change either the First Folio's wording or its punctuation so that meaning

---

*We have also consulted the computerized text of the First Folio provided by the Text Archive of the Oxford University Computing Centre, to which we are grateful.

changes, we list the change in the textual notes at the back of the book, even if all we have done is fix an obvious error.

We correct or regularize a number of the proper names in the dialogue and in the stage directions, as is the usual practice in editions of the play. For example, the Folio's spelling "Murellus" is changed to "Marullus"; the occasional appearance of "Antonio" in the Folio is regularized to "Antonius"; and there are a number of other comparable adjustments in the names. Since no scholars believe that the Folio *Julius Caesar* was printed directly from Shakespeare's manuscript, it would be difficult to identify the Folio's spellings of names as Shakespeare's personal preferences.

This edition differs from many earlier ones in its efforts to aid the reader in imagining the play as a performance. Thus stage directions are written with reference to the stage. For example, at 3.1.13, instead of providing a stage direction that says, "Caesar goes into the Capitol," we have offered something that can be presented on stage, "Caesar goes forward, the rest following." Whenever it is reasonably certain, in our view, that a speech is accompanied by a particular action, we provide a stage direction describing the action. (Occasional exceptions to this rule occur when the action is so obvious that to add a stage direction would insult the reader.) Stage directions for the entrance of characters in mid-scene are, with rare exceptions, placed so that they immediately precede the characters' participation in the scene, even though these entrances may appear somewhat earlier in the early printed texts. Whenever we move a stage direction, we record this change in the textual notes. Latin stage directions (e.g., *Exeunt*) are translated into English (e.g., *They exit*).

We expand the often severely abbreviated forms of names used as speech headings in early printed texts into the full names of the characters. We also regularize the speakers' names in speech headings, using only a single designation for each character, even though the early printed texts sometimes use a variety of designations. Variations in the speech headings of the early printed texts are recorded in the textual notes.

In the present edition, as well, we mark with a dash any change of address within a speech, unless a stage direction intervenes. When the *-ed* ending of a word is to be pronounced, we mark it with an accent. Like editors for the past two centuries, we print metrically linked lines in the following way:

CASSIUS
    This, Decius Brutus.
    BRUTUS   He is welcome too.
                                               (2.1.104–5)

However, when there are a number of short verse-lines that can be linked in more than one way, we do not, with rare exceptions, indent any of them.

The Explanatory Notes

The notes that appear on the pages facing the text are designed to provide readers with the help that they may need to enjoy the play. Whenever the meaning of a word in the text is not readily accessible in a good contemporary dictionary, we offer the meaning in a note. Sometimes we provide a note even when the relevant meaning is to be found in the dictionary but when the word has acquired since Shakespeare's time other potentially confusing meanings. In our notes, we try to offer modern synonyms for Shakespeare's words. We also try to indicate to the reader the connection between the word in the play and the modern synonym. For example, Shakespeare sometimes uses the word *head* to mean "source," but, for modern readers, there may be no connection evident between these two words. We provide the connection by explaining Shakespeare's usage as follows: "**head:** fountainhead, source." On some occasions, a whole phrase or clause needs explanation. Then, if space allows, we rephrase in our own words the difficult passage, and add at the end synonyms for individual words in the passage. When scholars have been unable to determine the meaning of a word or phrase, we acknowledge the uncertainty. Biblical quotations are from the Geneva Bible (1560), with spelling modernized.

The Tragedy of

JULIUS CAESAR

A faire corps as could be. *Alexander* left *Roxane* great with childe, for the which the MACEDO-
NIANS did her great honor: but she did malice *Statira* extreamely,& did finely deceiue her by
a counterfeat letter she sent,as if it had comen from *Alexander*,willing her to come vnto him.
But when she was come, *Roxane* killed her and her sister, and then threw their bodies into a   *Statira slaine*
well,and filled it vp wtth earth,by *Perdiccas* helpe and consent. *Perdiccas* came to be king, im-   *by Roxane.*
mediatly after *Alexanders* death, by meanes of *Arideus*, whom he kept about him for his gard
and safety.This *Arideus*, beeing borne of a common strumpet and common woman, called   *Arideus, A-*
Philinna,was halfe lunaticke,not by nature nor by chaunce:but,as it is reported,put out of his   *lexanders ba-*
wits when he was a yo·ng towardly boy, by drinkes, which *Olympias* caused to be geuen him,   *stard brother.*
and thereby continued franticke.

B

The end of Alexanders life.

THE LIFE OF
Iulius Cæsar.

C

D

A T what time *Sylla* was made Lord of all, he would haue had *Cæsar* put   *Cæsar ioyned*
away his wife *Cornelia*, the daughter of *Cinna* Dictator : but when he   *with Cinna &*
saw, he could neither with any promise nor threate bring him to it,he   *Marius.*
tooke her ioynter away from him.The cause of *Cæsars* ill will vnto *Sylla*,
E   was by meanes of mariage:for *Marius* thelder,maried his fathers own
sister, by whom he had *Marius* the younger,whereby *Cæsar* & he were
cosin germaines. *Sylla* being troubled in waightie matters, putting to
death so many of his enemies,when he came to be cõqueror, he made
no reckoning of *Cæsar*:but he was not contented to be hidden in safety,
but came and made sute vnto the people for the Priesthoodshippe that was voyde , when he
had scant any heare on his face. Howbeit he was repulsed by *Syllaes* meanes, that secretly was
against him.Who,when he was determined to haue killed him,some of his frendes told him,
that it was to no purpose to put so young a boy as he to death.But *Sylla* told them againe,that
they did not consider that there were many *Marians* in that young boy. *Cæsar* vnderstanding
F   that, stale out of ROME, and hidde him selfe a long time in the contrie of the SABINES, wan-
dring still from place to place. But one day being caried from house to house, he fell into the
handes of *Syllaes* souldiers, who searched all those places, and tooke them whom they found
SSS iiij

Title page of "The Life of Julius Caesar."
From Plutarch, *Lives of the Noble Grecians and Romanes* . . . (1579).

Characters in the Play

JULIUS CAESAR
CALPHURNIA, his wife
Servant to them

MARCUS BRUTUS
PORTIA, his wife
LUCIUS, their servant

CAIUS CASSIUS
CASCA
CINNA
DECIUS BRUTUS   } *patricians who, with Brutus,*
CAIUS LIGARIUS   *conspire against Caesar*
METELLUS CIMBER
TREBONIUS

CICERO
PUBLIUS   } *senators*
POPILIUS LENA

FLAVIUS   } *tribunes*
MARULLUS

MARK ANTONY
LEPIDUS   } *rulers of Rome in Acts 4 and 5*
OCTAVIUS
Servant to Antony
Servant to Octavius

3

LUCILIUS
TITINIUS
MESSALA
VARRO
CLAUDIUS
Young CATO   *officers and soldiers in the*
STRATO   *armies of Brutus and Cassius*
VOLUMNIUS
LABEO (nonspeaking)
FLAVIUS (nonspeaking)
DARDANUS
CLITUS

A Carpenter
A Cobbler
A Soothsayer
ARTEMIDORUS
First, Second, Third, and Fourth Plebeians
CINNA the Poet
PINDARUS, slave to Cassius, freed upon Cassius's death
First, Second, Third, and Fourth Soldiers in Brutus's
    army
Another Poet
A Messenger
First and Second Soldiers in Antony's army
Citizens, Senators, Petitioners, Plebeians, Soldiers

The Tragedy of

JULIUS CAESAR

ACT 1

1.1 In Rome the people are taking a holiday to celebrate the triumphant return of Julius Caesar. The tribunes Marullus and Flavius try to shame the people into returning to their places of work by reminding them how much they loved Caesar's rival Pompey, whom Caesar has destroyed and whose sons he has just defeated.

---

3. **mechanical:** workers
4–5. **sign / Of your profession:** distinctive clothes or insignia that indicate your trade
10. **in respect of:** compared with
11. **cobbler:** (1) bungler; (2) shoemaker (Marullus and Flavius think he means "bungler"; only at line 23 does Flavius understand that the "cobbler" is, in fact, a shoemaker.)
12. **directly:** straightforwardly
13. **use:** engage in, practice
15. **soles:** Because this word sounds the same as *souls*, the confusion introduced at line 11 continues.
16. **naughty:** good-for-nothing; impertinent

ACT 1

Scene 1

Enter Flavius, Marullus, and certain Commoners,
⌐including a Carpenter and a Cobbler,¬ over the stage.

FLAVIUS
    Hence! Home, you idle creatures, get you home!
    Is this a holiday? What, know you not,
    Being mechanical, you ought not walk
    Upon a laboring day without the sign
    Of your profession?—Speak, what trade art thou?   5
CARPENTER Why, sir, a carpenter.
MARULLUS
    Where is thy leather apron and thy rule?
    What dost thou with thy best apparel on?—
    You, sir, what trade are you?
COBBLER Truly, sir, in respect of a fine workman, I am   10
    but, as you would say, a cobbler.
MARULLUS
    But what trade art thou? Answer me directly.
COBBLER A trade, sir, that I hope I may use with a safe
    conscience, which is indeed, sir, a mender of bad
    soles.   15
FLAVIUS
    What trade, thou knave? Thou naughty knave, what
    trade?

7

18. **out:** out of temper, angry

19. **out:** (1) perplexed, disturbed; (2) worn out (i.e., wearing shoes with worn-out soles)

25. **meddle:** concern myself, deal

26. **withal:** nevertheless (pun on "**with awl**")

28. **recover:** (1) cure; (2) mend; **proper:** fine, respectable

29. **neat's leather:** cowhide; **gone:** walked

30. **wherefore:** why

35. **triumph:** triumphal procession (Caesar had overthrown the sons of **Pompey** [line 42], and the procession celebrated this victory.)

37. **tributaries:** those paying tribute, a tax exacted from a subject by a conqueror

39. **senseless:** insensate, blockish

42. **Pompey:** Pompey the Great, a Roman general and consul, defeated by Caesar and later murdered (See picture, below.)

47. **pass:** go through, traverse

48. **but:** only

Pompey the Great.
From [Guillaume Rouillé,] . . . *Promptuarii iconum* . . . (1553).

COBBLER Nay, I beseech you, sir, be not out with me.
Yet if you be out, sir, I can mend you.

MARULLUS
What mean'st thou by that? Mend me, thou saucy   20
fellow?

COBBLER Why, sir, cobble you.

FLAVIUS Thou art a cobbler, art thou?

COBBLER Truly, sir, all that I live by is with the
awl. I meddle with no tradesman's matters nor   25
women's matters, but withal I am indeed, sir, a
surgeon to old shoes: when they are in great danger,
I recover them. As proper men as ever trod upon
neat's leather have gone upon my handiwork.

FLAVIUS
But wherefore art not in thy shop today?   30
Why dost thou lead these men about the streets?

COBBLER Truly, sir, to wear out their shoes, to
get myself into more work. But indeed, sir, we
make holiday to see Caesar and to rejoice in his
triumph.   35

MARULLUS
Wherefore rejoice? What conquest brings he home?
What tributaries follow him to Rome
To grace in captive bonds his chariot wheels?
You blocks, you stones, you worse than senseless
things!   40
O you hard hearts, you cruel men of Rome,
Knew you not Pompey? Many a time and oft
Have you climbed up to walls and battlements,
To towers and windows, yea, to chimney tops,
Your infants in your arms, and there have sat   45
The livelong day, with patient expectation,
To see great Pompey pass the streets of Rome.
And when you saw his chariot but appear,
Have you not made an universal shout,
That Tiber trembled underneath her banks   50

51. **replication:** echo
54. **cull out:** select, pick out
56. **Pompey's blood:** the sons of Pompey
59. **intermit:** put off
62. **sort:** rank
63. **Tiber banks:** the banks of the **Tiber** River (See picture, pages xiv–xv.)
64–65. **till the lowest . . . of all:** i.e., until **the lowest stream** is made to crest at the river's highest bank   **most exalted:** highest
66. **See . . . moved:** i.e., note how the lowest of them is affected   **whe'er:** whether, if   **their basest mettle:** the most worthless spirit among them (**Mettle** and **metal** were used interchangeably.)   **moved:** emotionally touched
68. **Capitol:** national temple of Rome, dedicated to Jupiter, king of the Roman gods (See picture, page 14.)
69. **images:** i.e., statues
70. **ceremonies:** symbols of religious observance (In the next scene, we learn that these symbols are scarves.)
72. **feast of Lupercal:** an annual ceremony to honor Lupercus (the god Pan)
74. **about:** i.e., go about
75. **vulgar:** common people
76. **thick:** gathered in a mass
78. **pitch:** height (In falconry, the term indicates the highest point of the falcon's flight.)
79. **else:** otherwise

To hear the replication of your sounds
Made in her concave shores?
And do you now put on your best attire?
And do you now cull out a holiday?
And do you now strew flowers in his way   55
That comes in triumph over Pompey's blood?
Be gone!
Run to your houses, fall upon your knees,
Pray to the gods to intermit the plague
That needs must light on this ingratitude.   60
FLAVIUS
  Go, go, good countrymen, and for this fault
  Assemble all the poor men of your sort,
  Draw them to Tiber banks, and weep your tears
  Into the channel, till the lowest stream
  Do kiss the most exalted shores of all.   65
                              All the Commoners exit.
See whe'er their basest mettle be not moved.
They vanish tongue-tied in their guiltiness.
Go you down that way towards the Capitol.
This way will I. Disrobe the images
If you do find them decked with ceremonies.   70
MARULLUS May we do so?
  You know it is the feast of Lupercal.
FLAVIUS
  It is no matter. Let no images
  Be hung with Caesar's trophies. I'll about
  And drive away the vulgar from the streets;   75
  So do you too, where you perceive them thick.
  These growing feathers plucked from Caesar's wing
  Will make him fly an ordinary pitch,
  Who else would soar above the view of men
  And keep us all in servile fearfulness.   80
                      They exit ⌜in different directions.⌝

1.2 A soothsayer advises Caesar that the fifteenth of March will be a dangerous day for him. When Caesar and others exit, Cassius and Brutus remain behind. Cassius urges Brutus to oppose Caesar for fear that Caesar may become king. After Brutus and Cassius talk with Casca about Mark Antony's public offer of the crown to Caesar, Brutus agrees to continue his conversation with Cassius the next day. Cassius, alone at the end of the scene, expresses his surprise that Brutus, who is one of Caesar's favorites, is willing to conspire against Caesar and decides to take immediate advantage of this willingness.

---

0 SD. **for the course:** dressed **for the** race
10. **holy chase:** sacred race
11. **sterile curse:** curse of sterility
14. **Set on:** proceed
14 SD. **Sennet:** trumpet signal
18. **press:** crowd
21. **the ides of March:** i.e., **March** 15

Calphurnia.
From [Guillaume Rouillé,] . . . *Promptuarii iconum* . . . (1553).

⌜Scene 2⌝

Enter Caesar, Antony for the course, Calphurnia, Portia,
Decius, Cicero, Brutus, Cassius, Casca, a Soothsayer;
after them Marullus and Flavius ⌜and Commoners.⌝

CAESAR
  Calphurnia.
CASCA   Peace, ho! Caesar speaks.
CAESAR   Calphurnia.
CALPHURNIA Here, my lord.
CAESAR
  Stand you directly in Antonius' way   5
  When he doth run his course.—Antonius.
ANTONY Caesar, my lord.
CAESAR
  Forget not in your speed, Antonius,
  To touch Calphurnia, for our elders say
  The barren, touchèd in this holy chase,   10
  Shake off their sterile curse.
ANTONY   I shall remember.
  When Caesar says "Do this," it is performed.
CAESAR
  Set on and leave no ceremony out.   ⌜*Sennet.*⌝
SOOTHSAYER Caesar.   15
CAESAR Ha! Who calls?
CASCA
  Bid every noise be still. Peace, yet again!
CAESAR
  Who is it in the press that calls on me?
  I hear a tongue shriller than all the music
  Cry "Caesar." Speak. Caesar is turned to hear.   20
SOOTHSAYER
  Beware the ides of March.
CAESAR   What man is that?
BRUTUS
  A soothsayer bids you beware the ides of March.

30. **the order of the course:** i.e., **the** progress **of the** race

37. **of late:** lately

39. **was wont to:** used to

40. **stubborn and ... strange:** harsh and unfriendly (The image is from horsemanship.)

45. **Merely:** entirely

46. **passions of some difference:** conflicting emotions

47. **Conceptions ... myself:** strictly personal thoughts

48. **soil:** blemish

The Roman Capitol.
From Bartolommeo Marliani, *Urbis Romae topographia* ... (1588).

CAESAR
Set him before me. Let me see his face.
CASSIUS
Fellow, come from the throng.   25
                    ⌜*The Soothsayer comes forward.*⌝
                    Look upon Caesar.
CAESAR
What sayst thou to me now? Speak once again.
SOOTHSAYER   Beware the ides of March.
CAESAR
He is a dreamer. Let us leave him. Pass.
                    Sennet. All but Brutus and Cassius exit.
CASSIUS
Will you go see the order of the course?   30
BRUTUS   Not I.
CASSIUS   I pray you, do.
BRUTUS
I am not gamesome. I do lack some part
Of that quick spirit that is in Antony.
Let me not hinder, Cassius, your desires.   35
I'll leave you.
CASSIUS
Brutus, I do observe you now of late.
I have not from your eyes that gentleness
And show of love as I was wont to have.
You bear too stubborn and too strange a hand   40
Over your friend that loves you.
BRUTUS   Cassius,
Be not deceived. If I have veiled my look,
I turn the trouble of my countenance
Merely upon myself. Vexèd I am   45
Of late with passions of some difference,
Conceptions only proper to myself,
Which give some soil, perhaps, to my behaviors.
But let not therefore my good friends be grieved
(Among which number, Cassius, be you one)   50

51. **construe:** interpret (accent on first syllable)
54. **mistook your passion:** misinterpreted what you were feeling
55. **By means whereof:** and as a result
60. **just:** true
64. **shadow:** reflected image
65. **respect:** reputation
66. **Except:** i.e., always excepting
72. **Therefore:** as to that (question)
74. **glass:** looking **glass,** mirror
75. **modestly discover:** reveal without exaggeration
75–76. **to yourself . . . not of: to** you things about **yourself** that **you** do **not yet know**
77. **jealous on:** suspicious of; **gentle:** a complimentary epithet
78. **laughter:** butt of jokes, laughingstock; **did use:** were (I) accustomed
79. **stale:** make common and worthless
80. **protester:** one who protests (his friendship)
82. **scandal:** slander

Nor construe any further my neglect
Than that poor Brutus, with himself at war,
Forgets the shows of love to other men.

CASSIUS
Then, Brutus, I have much mistook your passion,
By means whereof this breast of mine hath buried   55
Thoughts of great value, worthy cogitations.
Tell me, good Brutus, can you see your face?

BRUTUS
No, Cassius, for the eye sees not itself
But by reflection, by some other things.

CASSIUS   'Tis just.   60
And it is very much lamented, Brutus,
That you have no such mirrors as will turn
Your hidden worthiness into your eye,
That you might see your shadow. I have heard
Where many of the best respect in Rome,   65
Except immortal Caesar, speaking of Brutus
And groaning underneath this age's yoke,
Have wished that noble Brutus had his eyes.

BRUTUS
Into what dangers would you lead me, Cassius,
That you would have me seek into myself   70
For that which is not in me?

CASSIUS
Therefore, good Brutus, be prepared to hear.
And since you know you cannot see yourself
So well as by reflection, I, your glass,
Will modestly discover to yourself   75
That of yourself which you yet know not of.
And be not jealous on me, gentle Brutus.
Were I a common laughter, or did use
To stale with ordinary oaths my love
To every new protester; if you know   80
That I do fawn on men and hug them hard
And after scandal them, or if you know

83. **profess myself:** i.e., **profess** friendship; **banqueting:** carousing

84. **rout:** crowd; **hold:** consider

84 SD. **Flourish:** a horn fanfare (usually accompanying ceremonial entrances and exits)

86. **Choose . . . king:** emphasis on **king**

90. **wherefore:** why

94. **indifferently:** impartially

95. **speed me:** make me prosper

98. **favor:** appearance

101. **single:** individual

102. **I had as lief not be: I had** just **as** soon **not live**

103. **such a thing . . . myself:** i.e., a man no better than I

108. **chafing with:** i.e., dashing against, as if in anger

110. **flood:** river

112. **Accoutered:** dressed

Cassius.
From [Guillaume Rouillé,] . . . *Promptuarii iconum* . . . (1553).

That I profess myself in banqueting
To all the rout, then hold me dangerous.

Flourish and shout.

BRUTUS
    What means this shouting? I do fear the people   85
    Choose Caesar for their king.
CASSIUS   Ay, do you fear it?
    Then must I think you would not have it so.
BRUTUS
    I would not, Cassius, yet I love him well.
    But wherefore do you hold me here so long?   90
    What is it that you would impart to me?
    If it be aught toward the general good,
    Set honor in one eye and death i' th' other
    And I will look on both indifferently;
    For let the gods so speed me as I love   95
    The name of honor more than I fear death.
CASSIUS
    I know that virtue to be in you, Brutus,
    As well as I do know your outward favor.
    Well, honor is the subject of my story.
    I cannot tell what you and other men   100
    Think of this life; but, for my single self,
    I had as lief not be as live to be
    In awe of such a thing as I myself.
    I was born free as Caesar; so were you;
    We both have fed as well, and we can both   105
    Endure the winter's cold as well as he.
    For once, upon a raw and gusty day,
    The troubled Tiber chafing with her shores,
    Caesar said to me "Dar'st thou, Cassius, now
    Leap in with me into this angry flood   110
    And swim to yonder point?" Upon the word,
    Accoutered as I was, I plungèd in
    And bade him follow; so indeed he did.
    The torrent roared, and we did buffet it

115. **lusty:** vigorous
116. **of controversy:** i.e., in rivalry with the waves and with each other
121. **Anchises:** the father of the Trojan hero **Aeneas** (See picture, below.)
127. **mark:** notice
130. **bend:** glance
131. **his:** its (i.e., the eye's)
133. **Mark:** pay attention to
135. **amaze:** astound
136. **temper:** constitution
137. **get the start of:** outdistance
138. **palm:** trophy for victory
143. **Colossus:** a gigantic bronze statue whose **legs,** according to legend, spanned the harbor at Rhodes (See picture, page 26.)
147. **our stars:** the **stars** that supposedly govern our lives

Aeneas and Anchises. (1.2.119–21)
From Geoffrey Whitney, *A choice of emblemes* . . . (1586).

With lusty sinews, throwing it aside   115
And stemming it with hearts of controversy.
But ere we could arrive the point proposed,
Caesar cried "Help me, Cassius, or I sink!"
I, as Aeneas, our great ancestor,
Did from the flames of Troy upon his shoulder   120
The old Anchises bear, so from the waves of Tiber
Did I the tired Caesar. And this man
Is now become a god, and Cassius is
A wretched creature and must bend his body
If Caesar carelessly but nod on him.   125
He had a fever when he was in Spain,
And when the fit was on him, I did mark
How he did shake. 'Tis true, this god did shake.
His coward lips did from their color fly,
And that same eye whose bend doth awe the world   130
Did lose his luster. I did hear him groan.
Ay, and that tongue of his that bade the Romans
Mark him and write his speeches in their books,
"Alas," it cried "Give me some drink, Titinius"
As a sick girl. You gods, it doth amaze me   135
A man of such a feeble temper should
So get the start of the majestic world
And bear the palm alone.
                                        Shout. Flourish.
BRUTUS Another general shout!
I do believe that these applauses are   140
For some new honors that are heaped on Caesar.
CASSIUS
Why, man, he doth bestride the narrow world
Like a Colossus, and we petty men
Walk under his huge legs and peep about
To find ourselves dishonorable graves.   145
Men at some time are masters of their fates.
The fault, dear Brutus, is not in our stars,
But in ourselves, that we are underlings.

156. **start:** i.e., conjure up (literally, force to leave its lair, a hunting term)
158. **meat:** food
159. **Age:** i.e., the present era
160. **breed ... bloods:** i.e., lineage of truly **noble** men
161. **the great flood:** in mythology, a **flood** that, in the far distant past, destroyed all of mankind except for one couple
168. **a Brutus once:** i.e., Lucius Junius **Brutus,** who, in legend, drove out the last of the ancient kings of Rome and founded the Roman Republic
168–70. **brooked ... king:** i.e., permitted the **devil** to reign **in Rome** as soon as allow **a king** to reign
171. **I am nothing jealous:** I have no doubt
172. **have some aim:** can guess
176. **moved:** urged
179. **Both meet:** suitable **both**

Brutus.
From [Guillaume Rouillé,] . . . *Promptuarii iconum* . . . (1553).

"Brutus" and "Caesar"—what should be in that
  "Caesar"?   150
Why should that name be sounded more than
  yours?
Write them together, yours is as fair a name;
Sound them, it doth become the mouth as well;
Weigh them, it is as heavy; conjure with 'em,   155
"Brutus" will start a spirit as soon as "Caesar."
Now, in the names of all the gods at once,
Upon what meat doth this our Caesar feed
That he is grown so great? Age, thou art shamed!
Rome, thou hast lost the breed of noble bloods!   160
When went there by an age, since the great flood,
But it was famed with more than with one man?
When could they say, till now, that talked of Rome,
That her wide walks encompassed but one man?
Now is it Rome indeed, and room enough   165
When there is in it but one only man.
O, you and I have heard our fathers say
There was a Brutus once that would have brooked
Th' eternal devil to keep his state in Rome
As easily as a king.   170
BRUTUS
That you do love me, I am nothing jealous.
What you would work me to, I have some aim.
How I have thought of this, and of these times,
I shall recount hereafter. For this present,
I would not, so with love I might entreat you,   175
Be any further moved. What you have said
I will consider; what you have to say
I will with patience hear, and find a time
Both meet to hear and answer such high things.
Till then, my noble friend, chew upon this: 180
Brutus had rather be a villager
Than to repute himself a son of Rome

184. **like:** likely
194. **chidden train:** scolded retinue
196. **ferret:** ferretlike (Ferrets' eyes are red.)
198. **crossed:** opposed
207. **well given:** well disposed

Ferret.
From Edward Topsell, *The historie of foure-footed beastes* . . . (1607).

Under these hard conditions as this time
Is like to lay upon us.
CASSIUS I am glad that my weak words   185
Have struck but thus much show of fire from
Brutus.

Enter Caesar and his train.

BRUTUS
The games are done, and Caesar is returning.
CASSIUS
As they pass by, pluck Casca by the sleeve,
And he will, after his sour fashion, tell you   190
What hath proceeded worthy note today.
BRUTUS
I will do so. But look you, Cassius,
The angry spot doth glow on Caesar's brow,
And all the rest look like a chidden train.
Calphurnia's cheek is pale, and Cicero   195
Looks with such ferret and such fiery eyes
As we have seen him in the Capitol,
Being crossed in conference by some senators.
CASSIUS
Casca will tell us what the matter is.
CAESAR Antonius.   200
ANTONY Caesar.
CAESAR
Let me have men about me that are fat,
Sleek-headed men, and such as sleep a-nights.
Yond Cassius has a lean and hungry look.
He thinks too much. Such men are dangerous.   205
ANTONY
Fear him not, Caesar; he's not dangerous.
He is a noble Roman, and well given.
CAESAR
Would he were fatter! But I fear him not.
Yet if my name were liable to fear,

215. **sort:** manner
216–17. **his spirit / That:** i.e., the **spirit** of anyone who
221. **rather tell thee: tell thee rather**
223. **on my right hand:** to my right-hand side
228. **sad:** serious
239. **marry:** i.e., indeed, to be sure; **was 't:** it was

Colossus. (1.2.143)
From André Thevet, *Cosmographie de Leuant* . . . (1554).

I do not know the man I should avoid   210
So soon as that spare Cassius. He reads much,
He is a great observer, and he looks
Quite through the deeds of men. He loves no plays,
As thou dost, Antony; he hears no music;
Seldom he smiles, and smiles in such a sort   215
As if he mocked himself and scorned his spirit
That could be moved to smile at anything.
Such men as he be never at heart's ease
Whiles they behold a greater than themselves,
And therefore are they very dangerous.   220
I rather tell thee what is to be feared
Than what I fear; for always I am Caesar.
Come on my right hand, for this ear is deaf,
And tell me truly what thou think'st of him.
                    Sennet. Caesar and his train exit
                    ⌜*but Casca remains behind.*⌝
CASCA You pulled me by the cloak. Would you speak   225
    with me?
BRUTUS
    Ay, Casca. Tell us what hath chanced today
    That Caesar looks so sad.
CASCA Why, you were with him, were you not?
BRUTUS
    I should not then ask Casca what had chanced.   230
CASCA Why, there was a crown offered him; and, being
    offered him, he put it by with the back of his hand,
    thus, and then the people fell a-shouting.
BRUTUS What was the second noise for?
CASCA Why, for that too.   235
CASSIUS
    They shouted thrice. What was the last cry for?
CASCA Why, for that too.
BRUTUS Was the crown offered him thrice?
CASCA Ay, marry, was 't, and he put it by thrice, every
    time gentler than other; and at every putting-by,   240
    mine honest neighbors shouted.

246. **mark:** pay attention to

250. **fain:** gladly

255. **chopped:** chapped

256. **nightcaps:** a possible reference to the felt cap *(pileus)* worn by ancient Greeks and Romans

262. **soft:** i.e., wait a minute

265. **'Tis very like:** it is quite likely; **falling sickness:** epilepsy (At line 267, Cassius puns on the term, saying, in effect, "It is we who are sick and falling.")

271. **use to do:** are accustomed to doing

CASSIUS Who offered him the crown?

CASCA Why, Antony.

BRUTUS
Tell us the manner of it, gentle Casca.

CASCA I can as well be hanged as tell the manner of it. 245
It was mere foolery; I did not mark it. I saw Mark
Antony offer him a crown (yet 'twas not a crown
neither; 'twas one of these coronets), and, as I told
you, he put it by once; but for all that, to my
thinking, he would fain have had it. Then he offered 250
it to him again; then he put it by again; but to my
thinking, he was very loath to lay his fingers off it.
And then he offered it the third time. He put it the
third time by, and still as he refused it the rabble-
ment hooted and clapped their chopped hands and 255
threw up their sweaty nightcaps and uttered such a
deal of stinking breath because Caesar refused the
crown that it had almost choked Caesar, for he
swooned and fell down at it. And for mine own part,
I durst not laugh for fear of opening my lips and 260
receiving the bad air.

CASSIUS
But soft, I pray you. What, did Caesar swoon?

CASCA He fell down in the marketplace and foamed at
mouth and was speechless.

BRUTUS
'Tis very like; he hath the falling sickness. 265

CASSIUS
No, Caesar hath it not; but you and I
And honest Casca, we have the falling sickness.

CASCA I know not what you mean by that, but I am
sure Caesar fell down. If the tag-rag people did not
clap him and hiss him, according as he pleased and 270
displeased them, as they use to do the players in the
theater, I am no true man.

276. **plucked me ope:** plucked open; **doublet:** a close-fitting (Elizabethan) jacket (See picture, below.)

277. **An:** if

277–78. **man . . . occupation:** i.e., working **man,** tradesman

278. **at a word: at** his **word**

279. **would I might:** wish **I might**

297. **put to silence:** silenced (i.e., removed from office or perhaps imprisoned)

Two Elizabethans wearing doublets. (1.2.276)
From Robert Greene, *A quip for an vpstart courtier . . .* (1620).

BRUTUS
What said he when he came unto himself?

CASCA Marry, before he fell down, when he perceived
the common herd was glad he refused the crown, 275
he plucked me ope his doublet and offered them his
throat to cut. An I had been a man of any occupation, if I would not have taken him at a word, I
would I might go to hell among the rogues. And so
he fell. When he came to himself again, he said if he 280
had done or said anything amiss, he desired their
Worships to think it was his infirmity. Three or four
wenches where I stood cried "Alas, good soul!" and
forgave him with all their hearts. But there's no
heed to be taken of them; if Caesar had stabbed 285
their mothers, they would have done no less.

BRUTUS
And, after that, he came thus sad away?

CASCA Ay.

CASSIUS Did Cicero say anything?

CASCA Ay, he spoke Greek. 290

CASSIUS To what effect?

CASCA Nay, an I tell you that, I'll ne'er look you i' th'
face again. But those that understood him smiled at
one another and shook their heads. But for mine
own part, it was Greek to me. I could tell you more 295
news too: Marullus and Flavius, for pulling scarves
off Caesar's images, are put to silence. Fare you
well. There was more foolery yet, if I could remember it.

CASSIUS Will you sup with me tonight, Casca? 300

CASCA No, I am promised forth.

CASSIUS Will you dine with me tomorrow?

CASCA Ay, if I be alive, and your mind hold, and your
dinner worth the eating.

CASSIUS Good. I will expect you. 305

CASCA Do so. Farewell both. *He exits.*

308. **quick mettle:** sharp, lively spirited   **quick:** alive

311. **However: however** much; **puts on...** **form:** adopts this apparently stupid manner

313. **stomach:** desire, inclination (with a pun on the word's primary meaning)

321. **mettle:** (1) spirit; (2) substance (metal); **wrought:** shaped, fashioned

322. **From that it is disposed:** i.e., away from the way **it is** constituted; **meet:** appropriate

323. **their likes:** those who are like them

325. **bear me hard:** resent me

327. **humor me:** influence me (as I have done him)

328. **hands:** handwritings; **his:** Brutus's

332. **glancèd at:** i.e., mentioned

333. **seat him sure: seat** himself securely

BRUTUS
　What a blunt fellow is this grown to be!
　He was quick mettle when he went to school.
CASSIUS
　So is he now in execution
　Of any bold or noble enterprise,   310
　However he puts on this tardy form.
　This rudeness is a sauce to his good wit,
　Which gives men stomach to digest his words
　With better appetite.
BRUTUS
　And so it is. For this time I will leave you.   315
　Tomorrow, if you please to speak with me,
　I will come home to you; or, if you will,
　Come home to me, and I will wait for you.
CASSIUS
　I will do so. Till then, think of the world.
　　　　　　　　　　　　　　　　　Brutus exits.
　Well, Brutus, thou art noble. Yet I see   320
　Thy honorable mettle may be wrought
　From that it is disposed. Therefore it is meet
　That noble minds keep ever with their likes;
　For who so firm that cannot be seduced?
　Caesar doth bear me hard, but he loves Brutus.   325
　If I were Brutus now, and he were Cassius,
　He should not humor me. I will this night
　In several hands in at his windows throw,
　As if they came from several citizens,
　Writings, all tending to the great opinion   330
　That Rome holds of his name, wherein obscurely
　Caesar's ambition shall be glancèd at
　And after this, let Caesar seat him sure,
　For we will shake him, or worse days endure.
　　　　　　　　　　　　　　　　　　He exits.

1.3 Casca, meeting Cicero, describes the marvels visible in the streets that night and suggests that the marvels foretell important events to come. Cicero having left, Cassius arrives to persuade Casca to join the conspiracy to liberate Rome from the threat of Caesar's kingship. When Cinna joins them, Cassius sends him to leave letters where Brutus may find them and be persuaded that his opposition to Caesar is desired by many.

---

   1. **even:** evening
   3. **moved:** troubled, perturbed
   18. **sensible of:** feeling, affected by
   19. **ha':** have; **put up:** sheathed
   20. **Against:** in front of
   21. **glazed:** stared
   22. **annoying:** harming
   22–23. **drawn / Upon a heap:** gathered in a crowd
   23. **ghastly:** pale, wan
   26. **bird of night:** screech owl (See picture, page 40.)
   28. **prodigies:** extraordinary events; omens
   29. **conjointly meet:** occur simultaneously

⌜Scene 3⌝

Thunder and lightning. Enter Casca and Cicero.

CICERO
Good even, Casca. Brought you Caesar home?
Why are you breathless? And why stare you so?
CASCA
Are not you moved, when all the sway of earth
Shakes like a thing unfirm? O Cicero,
I have seen tempests when the scolding winds   5
Have rived the knotty oaks, and I have seen
Th' ambitious ocean swell and rage and foam
To be exalted with the threat'ning clouds;
But never till tonight, never till now,
Did I go through a tempest dropping fire.   10
Either there is a civil strife in heaven,
Or else the world, too saucy with the gods,
Incenses them to send destruction.
CICERO
Why, saw you anything more wonderful?
CASCA
A common slave (you know him well by sight)   15
Held up his left hand, which did flame and burn
Like twenty torches joined; and yet his hand,
Not sensible of fire, remained unscorched.
Besides (I ha' not since put up my sword),
Against the Capitol I met a lion,   20
Who glazed upon me and went surly by
Without annoying me. And there were drawn
Upon a heap a hundred ghastly women,
Transformèd with their fear, who swore they saw
Men all in fire walk up and down the streets.   25
And yesterday the bird of night did sit
Even at noonday upon the marketplace,
Hooting and shrieking. When these prodigies
Do so conjointly meet, let not men say

32. **climate:** i.e., region

33. **strange-disposèd:** extraordinary, abnormal

34. **construe:** interpret (accent on first syllable)

35. **Clean from the purpose of:** in a way entirely different **from the** meaning **of**

45. **what night is this:** i.e., **what** a **night this is**!

51. **unbracèd:** i.e., with doublet unfastened (See picture of doublets, page 30.)

52. **thunder-stone:** stones thought to be released in thunder and lightning

53. **cross:** crisscrossing

An earthquake: "The sway of earth shakes like a thing unfirm." (1.3.3–4)

From Conrad Lycosthenes, *Prodigiorum* . . . (1557).

"These are their reasons, they are natural,"   30
For I believe they are portentous things
Unto the climate that they point upon.
CICERO
Indeed, it is a strange-disposèd time.
But men may construe things after their fashion,
Clean from the purpose of the things themselves.   35
Comes Caesar to the Capitol tomorrow?
CASCA
He doth, for he did bid Antonius
Send word to you he would be there tomorrow.
CICERO
Good night then, Casca. This disturbèd sky
Is not to walk in.   40
CASCA   Farewell, Cicero   *Cicero exits.*

Enter Cassius.

CASSIUS Who's there?
CASCA   A Roman.
CASSIUS   Casca, by your voice.
CASCA
Your ear is good. Cassius, what night is this!   45
CASSIUS
A very pleasing night to honest men.
CASCA
Who ever knew the heavens menace so?
CASSIUS
Those that have known the earth so full of faults.
For my part, I have walked about the streets,
Submitting me unto the perilous night,   50
And thus unbracèd, Casca, as you see,
Have bared my bosom to the thunder-stone;
And when the cross blue lightning seemed to open
The breast of heaven, I did present myself
Even in the aim and very flash of it.   55

56. **wherefore:** why
58. **tokens:** ominous signs
59. **astonish:** stun with fear
61. **want:** lack
67. **from quality and kind:** i.e., (act in a way) contrary to nature
68. **calculate:** reckon, make calculations
69–71. **change . . . quality: change from their** natural states to an extraordinary condition **ordinance:** established order **preformèd faculties:** previously formed properties
74. **monstrous state:** unnatural realm or government
81. **fearful:** frightening; **eruptions:** violent outbursts of nature
84. **thews:** sinews
85. **woe the while:** alas for the age; **fathers' minds:** i.e., ancestors' manly spirits
87. **yoke and sufferance:** i.e., patient submission to the **yoke** of servitude

CASCA

But wherefore did you so much tempt the heavens?
It is the part of men to fear and tremble
When the most mighty gods by tokens send
Such dreadful heralds to astonish us.

CASSIUS

You are dull, Casca, and those sparks of life   60
That should be in a Roman you do want,
Or else you use not. You look pale, and gaze,
And put on fear, and cast yourself in wonder,
To see the strange impatience of the heavens.
But if you would consider the true cause   65
Why all these fires, why all these gliding ghosts,
Why birds and beasts from quality and kind,
Why old men, fools, and children calculate,
Why all these things change from their ordinance,
Their natures, and preformèd faculties,   70
To monstrous quality—why, you shall find
That heaven hath infused them with these spirits
To make them instruments of fear and warning
Unto some monstrous state.
Now could I, Casca, name to thee a man   75
Most like this dreadful night,
That thunders, lightens, opens graves, and roars
As doth the lion in the Capitol;
A man no mightier than thyself or me
In personal action, yet prodigious grown,   80
And fearful, as these strange eruptions are.

CASCA

'Tis Caesar that you mean, is it not, Cassius?

CASSIUS

Let it be who it is. For Romans now
Have thews and limbs like to their ancestors.
But, woe the while, our fathers' minds are dead,   85
And we are governed with our mothers' spirits.
Our yoke and sufferance show us womanish.

95. **Therein:** i.e., in giving men power to take their own lives

96. **Nor . . . nor:** neither . . . **nor**

98. **Can . . . spirit: can** hold or confine a resolute mind

99. **bars:** barriers

100. **dismiss:** let go of, free

103 SD. **still:** i.e., continues

105. **bondman:** slave

110. **hinds:** deer; servants

114. **base matter:** i.e., kindling, fuel; **illuminate:** set alight; make illustrious

118. **My answer must be made:** i.e., I **must** answer for what I have said

119. **are . . . indifferent:** make no difference **to me**

A screech owl. (1.3.26–28)
From Konrad Gesner, *Icones animalium quadrupedum* . . . (1560).

CASCA
Indeed, they say the Senators tomorrow
Mean to establish Caesar as a king,
And he shall wear his crown by sea and land   90
In every place save here in Italy.
CASSIUS
I know where I will wear this dagger then;
Cassius from bondage will deliver Cassius.
Therein, you gods, you make the weak most strong;
Therein, you gods, you tyrants do defeat.   95
Nor stony tower, nor walls of beaten brass,
Nor airless dungeon, nor strong links of iron,
Can be retentive to the strength of spirit;
But life, being weary of these worldly bars,
Never lacks power to dismiss itself.   100
If I know this, know all the world besides,
That part of tyranny that I do bear
I can shake off at pleasure.   *Thunder still.*
CASCA   So can I.
So every bondman in his own hand bears   105
The power to cancel his captivity.
CASSIUS
And why should Caesar be a tyrant, then?
Poor man, I know he would not be a wolf
But that he sees the Romans are but sheep;
He were no lion, were not Romans hinds.   110
Those that with haste will make a mighty fire
Begin it with weak straws. What trash is Rome,
What rubbish, and what offal when it serves
For the base matter to illuminate
So vile a thing as Caesar! But, O grief,   115
Where hast thou led me? I perhaps speak this
Before a willing bondman; then, I know
My answer must be made. But I am armed,
And dangers are to me indifferent.

121. **fleering:** obsequiously smiling; **Hold:** i.e., here, take it

122. **factious:** active in the faction (against Caesar)

126. **moved:** persuaded

130. **by this:** i.e., by now, by this time

131. **Pompey's Porch:** the portico or colonnade adjoining Pompey's Theater, built by Pompey during his second consulship (See pictures, page xv and below.)

133. **element:** sky

134. **favor 's:** appearance is

136. **close:** hidden

140–41. **incorporate / To:** closely united with

141. **stayed for:** waited for

142. **on 't:** i.e., of it

Pompey's Theater and Pompey's "Porch."
From Alessandro Donati, . . . *Roma* . . . (1694).

CASCA

You speak to Casca, and to such a man   120
That is no fleering telltale. Hold. My hand.
                              ⌜*They shake hands.*⌝
Be factious for redress of all these griefs,
And I will set this foot of mine as far
As who goes farthest.

CASSIUS   There's a bargain made.   125
Now know you, Casca, I have moved already
Some certain of the noblest-minded Romans
To undergo with me an enterprise
Of honorable-dangerous consequence.
And I do know by this they stay for me   130
In Pompey's Porch. For now, this fearful night,
There is no stir or walking in the streets;
And the complexion of the element
⌜In⌝ favor 's like the work we have in hand,
Most bloody, fiery, and most terrible.   135

Enter Cinna.

CASCA

Stand close awhile, for here comes one in haste.

CASSIUS

'Tis Cinna; I do know him by his gait.
He is a friend.—Cinna, where haste you so?

CINNA

To find out you. Who's that? Metellus Cimber?

CASSIUS

No, it is Casca, one incorporate   140
To our attempts. Am I not stayed for, Cinna?

CINNA

I am glad on 't. What a fearful night is this!
There's two or three of us have seen strange sights.

CASSIUS   Am I not stayed for? Tell me.

CINNA

Yes, you are. O Cassius, if you could   145
But win the noble Brutus to our party—

148. **Praetor's chair:** the seat from which Brutus, as chief praetor (the position just below consul), dispensed judgments on civil offenses

151. **old Brutus' statue:** the **statue** of Lucius Junius Brutus (See note to 1.2.168.)

152. **Repair:** go

155. **hie:** hurry

159. **Three parts:** three-quarters

161. **yields him ours:** i.e., will deliver himself to us

163–65. **And that which ... worthiness:** i.e., and his support will, in the eyes of the people, transform our questionable actions into honorable deeds **countenance:** approval; also, (noble) appearance **alchemy:** the "science" of transmuting base metals into gold

167. **conceited:** conceived

CASSIUS, ⌜*handing him papers*⌝
  Be you content. Good Cinna, take this paper,
  And look you lay it in the Praetor's chair,
  Where Brutus may but find it; and throw this
  In at his window; set this up with wax   150
  Upon old Brutus' statue. All this done,
  Repair to Pompey's Porch, where you shall find us.
  Is Decius Brutus and Trebonius there?
CINNA
  All but Metellus Cimber, and he's gone
  To seek you at your house. Well, I will hie   155
  And so bestow these papers as you bade me.
CASSIUS
  That done, repair to Pompey's Theater.
                                         Cinna exits.
  Come, Casca, you and I will yet ere day
  See Brutus at his house. Three parts of him
  Is ours already, and the man entire   160
  Upon the next encounter yields him ours.
CASCA
  O, he sits high in all the people's hearts,
  And that which would appear offense in us
  His countenance, like richest alchemy,
  Will change to virtue and to worthiness.   165
CASSIUS
  Him and his worth and our great need of him
  You have right well conceited. Let us go,
  For it is after midnight, and ere day
  We will awake him and be sure of him.
                                         They exit.

The Tragedy of

JULIUS CAESAR

ACT 2

2.1 Brutus anxiously ponders joining the conspiracy against Caesar. When he is brought one of the unsigned letters that Cassius has had left for him to find, Brutus decides to act. Visited by the conspirators, he agrees to join them but rejects their plan to kill Mark Antony as well as Caesar. When the other conspirators have left, Portia, Brutus's wife, begs of him an explanation for his sudden change of mood. Brutus, joined by Caius Ligarius, departs for Caesar's.

---

0 SD. **orchard:** garden (See picture, page 50.)

4. **fault:** frailty

11. **spurn:** i.e., strike out (literally, kick)

12. **the general:** i.e., **the general** good; **would be:** wishes to be

16. **craves:** demands; **Crown him that:** perhaps, **crown him** as king or emperor

17. **sting:** fang, venom tooth

ACT 2

⌜Scene 1⌝

Enter Brutus in his orchard.

BRUTUS What, Lucius, ho!—
I cannot by the progress of the stars
Give guess how near to day.—Lucius, I say!—
I would it were my fault to sleep so soundly.—
When, Lucius, when? Awake, I say! What, Lucius! 5

Enter Lucius.

LUCIUS Called you, my lord?
BRUTUS
Get me a taper in my study, Lucius.
When it is lighted, come and call me here.
LUCIUS I will, my lord.   *He exits.*
BRUTUS
It must be by his death. And for my part   10
I know no personal cause to spurn at him,
But for the general. He would be crowned:
How that might change his nature, there's the
  question.
It is the bright day that brings forth the adder,   15
And that craves wary walking. Crown him that,
And then I grant we put a sting in him
That at his will he may do danger with.
Th' abuse of greatness is when it disjoins

49

20. **Remorse:** compassion

21. **affections:** feelings, desires; **swayed:** influenced (him)

22. **proof:** experience

23. **lowliness:** humility

25. **round:** rung (of **the ladder**)

27. **base degrees:** lower rungs or steps

29. **prevent:** forestall, anticipate

29–30. **since the quarrel . . . he is:** i.e., **since the** case against Caesar is not plausible in terms of his present behavior   **quarrel:** cause of complaint

31. **Fashion it:** i.e., make the case

34. **as his kind:** i.e., as is natural for a serpent

35. **mischievous:** harmful

37. **closet:** private room, **study** (line 7)

46. **exhalations:** meteors

Orchard. (2.1.0 SD)
From Octavio Boldoni, *Theatrum temporaneum* . . . (1636).

Remorse from power. And, to speak truth of Caesar,   20
I have not known when his affections swayed
More than his reason. But 'tis a common proof
That lowliness is young ambition's ladder,
Whereto the ⌐climber-upward¬ turns his face;
But, when he once attains the upmost round,   25
He then unto the ladder turns his back,
Looks in the clouds, scorning the base degrees
By which he did ascend. So Caesar may.
Then, lest he may, prevent. And since the quarrel
Will bear no color for the thing he is,   30
Fashion it thus: that what he is, augmented,
Would run to these and these extremities.
And therefore think him as a serpent's egg,
Which, hatched, would, as his kind, grow
   mischievous,   35
And kill him in the shell.

Enter Lucius.

LUCIUS
The taper burneth in your closet, sir.
Searching the window for a flint, I found
This paper, thus sealed up, and I am sure
It did not lie there when I went to bed.   40
                  Gives him the letter.

BRUTUS
Get you to bed again. It is not day.
Is not tomorrow, boy, the ⌐ides¬ of March?
LUCIUS   I know not, sir.
BRUTUS
Look in the calendar, and bring me word.
LUCIUS   I will, sir.   *He exits.*   45
BRUTUS
The exhalations, whizzing in the air,
Give so much light that I may read by them.
            Opens the letter and reads.

53. **piece it out:** fill in what has been left unsaid

56–57. **My . . . king:** See note to 1.2.168, and picture, page 54.   **The Tarquin:** i.e., Tarquinius Superbus, the last **king** of **Rome**

59–61. **I make . . . Brutus:** i.e., I promise that if **redress** (from tyranny) does **follow** my actions (of speaking and striking), **Rome** will receive all that she has asked from **Brutus**

62 SD. **within:** offstage

67. **motion:** proposal (of the action)

68. **phantasma:** nightmare

69–70. **The genius and the mortal instruments . . . council:** In classical thought, each man was born with an attendant spirit (his *daemon*, or **genius**). Brutus may be saying that this attendant spirit is taking counsel with the human body, or, more generally, that the man's soul or self is consulting with his body.   **mortal instruments:** the physical agents that carry out the action

73. **brother:** brother-in-law (Cassius was married to Brutus's sister.)

Brutus, thou sleep'st. Awake, and see thyself!
Shall Rome, etc. Speak, strike, redress!
"Brutus, thou sleep'st. Awake."   50
Such instigations have been often dropped
Where I have took them up.
"Shall Rome, etc." Thus must I piece it out:
Shall Rome stand under one man's awe? What,
    Rome?   55
My ancestors did from the streets of Rome
The Tarquin drive when he was called a king.
"Speak, strike, redress!" Am I entreated
To speak and strike? O Rome, I make thee promise,
If the redress will follow, thou receivest   60
Thy full petition at the hand of Brutus.

Enter Lucius.

LUCIUS   Sir, March is wasted fifteen days.
                                  Knock within.
BRUTUS
'Tis good. Go to the gate; somebody knocks.
                              ⌜*Lucius exits.*⌝
Since Cassius first did whet me against Caesar,
I have not slept.   65
Between the acting of a dreadful thing
And the first motion, all the interim is
Like a phantasma or a hideous dream.
The genius and the mortal instruments
Are then in council, and the state of man,   70
Like to a little kingdom, suffers then
The nature of an insurrection.

Enter Lucius.

LUCIUS
Sir, 'tis your brother Cassius at the door,
Who doth desire to see you.

81. **discover:** identify
82. **any mark of favor:** i.e., **any** of their features
91. **if thou path . . . on:** if you walk without disguise
92. **Erebus:** a place of darkness between Earth and Hades
93. **prevention:** being forestalled
94. **upon:** in intruding upon
95. **Good morrow: good** morning

Brutus's ancestors driving out "the Tarquin."
(2.1.56–57)
From Livy, *Historicus duobus libris auctos* . . . (1520).

BRUTUS   Is he alone?   75
LUCIUS
  No, sir. There are more with him.
BRUTUS   Do you know
    them?
LUCIUS
  No, sir. Their hats are plucked about their ears,
  And half their faces buried in their cloaks,   80
  That by no means I may discover them
  By any mark of favor.
BRUTUS   Let 'em enter.   ⌜*Lucius exits.*⌝
  They are the faction. O conspiracy,
  Sham'st thou to show thy dang'rous brow by night,   85
  When evils are most free? O, then, by day
  Where wilt thou find a cavern dark enough
  To mask thy monstrous visage? Seek none,
    conspiracy.
  Hide it in smiles and affability;   90
  For if thou path, thy native semblance on,
  Not Erebus itself were dim enough
  To hide thee from prevention.

Enter the conspirators, Cassius, Casca, Decius, Cinna,
Metellus, and Trebonius.

CASSIUS
  I think we are too bold upon your rest.
  Good morrow, Brutus. Do we trouble you?   95
BRUTUS
  I have been up this hour, awake all night.
  Know I these men that come along with you?
CASSIUS
  Yes, every man of them; and no man here
  But honors you, and every one doth wish
  You had but that opinion of yourself   100
  Which every noble Roman bears of you.
  This is Trebonius.

108. **watchful cares: cares** that keep you watching (i.e., awake)

114. **fret:** interlace with, as in fretwork

117. **growing on:** advancing toward

118. **Weighing:** i.e., in accord with (literally, considering, taking due account of); **the youthful ... year:** i.e., the fact that it is spring

121. **He:** i.e., the sun

122. **as the Capitol:** i.e., **as** does **the Capitol**

123. **all over:** i.e., every one of you

125. **face of men:** faces of our fellow citizens

126. **sufferance:** suffering

127. **betimes:** at once

129. **high-sighted:** haughty; **range:** stray freely

BRUTUS   He is welcome hither.
CASSIUS
   This, Decius Brutus.
BRUTUS   He is welcome too.   105
CASSIUS
   This, Casca; this, Cinna; and this, Metellus Cimber.
BRUTUS   They are all welcome.
   What watchful cares do interpose themselves
   Betwixt your eyes and night?
CASSIUS   Shall I entreat a word?   110
                 ⌜*Brutus and Cassius*⌝ *whisper.*
DECIUS
   Here lies the east; doth not the day break here?
CASCA   No.
CINNA
   O pardon, sir, it doth; and yon gray lines
   That fret the clouds are messengers of day.
CASCA
   You shall confess that you are both deceived.   115
   Here, as I point my sword, the sun arises,
   Which is a great way growing on the south,
   Weighing the youthful season of the year.
   Some two months hence, up higher toward the
      north   120
   He first presents his fire, and the high east
   Stands, as the Capitol, directly here.
BRUTUS, ⌜*coming forward with Cassius*⌝
   Give me your hands all over, one by one.
CASSIUS
   And let us swear our resolution.
BRUTUS
   No, not an oath. If not the face of men,   125
   The sufferance of our souls, the time's abuse—
   If these be motives weak, break off betimes,
   And every man hence to his idle bed.
   So let high-sighted tyranny range on

130. **drop by lottery:** i.e., die at the whim of a murderous tyrant; **these:** i.e., **these motives** (line 127)

135. **prick:** incite

136. **Than secret Romans:** i.e., **than** that of **Romans** who are discreet, who will not give away secrets

137. **palter:** waver, shift position

138. **honesty . . . engaged:** honor pledged to honor

139. **fall for:** die because of

140. **men cautelous: men** who are cautious, wary

141. **suffering:** long-suffering, patient

144. **even:** straightforward

145. **insuppressive:** irrepressible

146. **To think that or . . . or:** by thinking **that** either . . . **or**

149. **several:** individual, separate

152. **sound him:** i.e., find out his feelings

161. **gravity:** graveness, weighty dignity

Till each man drop by lottery. But if these—   130
As I am sure they do—bear fire enough
To kindle cowards and to steel with valor
The melting spirits of women, then, countrymen,
What need we any spur but our own cause
To prick us to redress? What other bond   135
Than secret Romans that have spoke the word
And will not palter? And what other oath
Than honesty to honesty engaged
That this shall be or we will fall for it?
Swear priests and cowards and men cautelous,   140
Old feeble carrions, and such suffering souls
That welcome wrongs; unto bad causes swear
Such creatures as men doubt; but do not stain
The even virtue of our enterprise,
Nor th' insuppressive mettle of our spirits,   145
To think that or our cause or our performance
Did need an oath, when every drop of blood
That every Roman bears, and nobly bears,
Is guilty of a several bastardy
If he do break the smallest particle   150
Of any promise that hath passed from him.
CASSIUS
But what of Cicero? Shall we sound him?
I think he will stand very strong with us.
CASCA
Let us not leave him out.
CINNA   No, by no means.   155
METELLUS
O, let us have him, for his silver hairs
Will purchase us a good opinion
And buy men's voices to commend our deeds.
It shall be said his judgment ruled our hands.
Our youths and wildness shall no whit appear,   160
But all be buried in his gravity.

162. **break with:** disclose our plans to
168. **meet:** fitting
170. **of him:** in him
171. **shrewd:** malicious
172. **improve:** put to good use
173. **annoy:** injure
177. **envy:** malice
182. **come by:** get at
184. **gentle:** honorable
189. **their servants:** i.e., our hands
191. **envious:** malicious, mean-spirited

BRUTUS
O, name him not! Let us not break with him,
For he will never follow anything
That other men begin.
CASSIUS Then leave him out.   165
CASCA Indeed, he is not fit.
DECIUS
Shall no man else be touched, but only Caesar?
CASSIUS
Decius, well urged. I think it is not meet
Mark Antony, so well beloved of Caesar,
Should outlive Caesar. We shall find of him   170
A shrewd contriver; and, you know, his means,
If he improve them, may well stretch so far
As to annoy us all; which to prevent,
Let Antony and Caesar fall together.
BRUTUS
Our course will seem too bloody, Caius Cassius,   175
To cut the head off and then hack the limbs,
Like wrath in death and envy afterwards;
For Antony is but a limb of Caesar.
Let's be sacrificers, but not butchers, Caius.
We all stand up against the spirit of Caesar,   180
And in the spirit of men there is no blood.
O, that we then could come by Caesar's spirit
And not dismember Caesar! But, alas,
Caesar must bleed for it. And, gentle friends,
Let's kill him boldly, but not wrathfully.   185
Let's carve him as a dish fit for the gods,
Not hew him as a carcass fit for hounds.
And let our hearts, as subtle masters do,
Stir up their servants to an act of rage
And after seem to chide 'em. This shall make   190
Our purpose necessary and not envious;
Which so appearing to the common eyes,
We shall be called purgers, not murderers.

198. **engrafted:** firmly established

201. **take thought:** grieve, give way to melancholy

202. **were much he should:** i.e., is more than can be expected of him

204. **no fear:** nothing to fear

213. **from the main opinion:** contrary to **the** forceful **opinion**

215. **apparent prodigies:** conspicuous omens

217. **augurers:** augurs (Roman religious officials whose function was to prophesy future events) See picture, page 76.

221. **unicorns . . . trees:** In Spenser's *Faerie Queene* (1590), a lion escapes an attack from a unicorn by tricking it into stabbing its horn into a tree. (See picture, page 64.)

222. **glasses:** mirrors; **holes:** pitfalls

223. **toils:** nets

And for Mark Antony, think not of him,
For he can do no more than Caesar's arm   195
When Caesar's head is off.
CASSIUS   Yet I fear him,
For in the engrafted love he bears to Caesar—
BRUTUS
Alas, good Cassius, do not think of him.
If he love Caesar, all that he can do   200
Is to himself: take thought and die for Caesar.
And that were much he should, for he is given
To sports, to wildness, and much company.
TREBONIUS
There is no fear in him. Let him not die,
For he will live and laugh at this hereafter.   205
                                        Clock strikes.
BRUTUS
Peace, count the clock.
CASSIUS   The clock hath stricken
three.
TREBONIUS
'Tis time to part.
CASSIUS   But it is doubtful yet   210
Whether Caesar will come forth today or no,
For he is superstitious grown of late,
Quite from the main opinion he held once
Of fantasy, of dreams, and ceremonies.
It may be these apparent prodigies,   215
The unaccustomed terror of this night,
And the persuasion of his augurers
May hold him from the Capitol today.
DECIUS
Never fear that. If he be so resolved,
I can o'ersway him, for he loves to hear   220
That unicorns may be betrayed with trees,
And bears with glasses, elephants with holes,
Lions with toils, and men with flatterers.

227. **humor:** mood; **bent:** direction, inclination
229. **fetch:** escort
230. **uttermost:** latest hour
232. **doth bear . . . hard:** resents, has a grudge against
233. **rated:** berated, rebuked harshly
235. **by him:** i.e., to him
238. **upon 's:** upon us
244. **put on:** i.e., reveal (literally, dress themselves in)
246. **formal constancy:** outward composure
250. **figures . . . fantasies:** imaginary forms or fancies

OF THE VNICORNE.

Unicorn. (2.1.221)
From Edward Topsell, *The historie of foure-footed beastes* . . . (1607).

But when I tell him he hates flatterers,
He says he does, being then most flatterèd.   225
Let me work,
For I can give his humor the true bent,
And I will bring him to the Capitol.

CASSIUS
Nay, we will all of us be there to fetch him.

BRUTUS
By the eighth hour, is that the uttermost?   230

CINNA
Be that the uttermost, and fail not then.

METELLUS
Caius Ligarius doth bear Caesar hard,
Who rated him for speaking well of Pompey.
I wonder none of you have thought of him.

BRUTUS
Now, good Metellus, go along by him.   235
He loves me well, and I have given him reasons.
Send him but hither, and I'll fashion him.

CASSIUS
The morning comes upon 's. We'll leave you,
    Brutus.
And, friends, disperse yourselves, but all remember   240
What you have said, and show yourselves true
    Romans.

BRUTUS
Good gentlemen, look fresh and merrily.
Let not our looks put on our purposes,
But bear it, as our Roman actors do,   245
With untired spirits and formal constancy.
And so good morrow to you every one.
                              All but Brutus exit.
Boy! Lucius!—Fast asleep? It is no matter.
Enjoy the honey-heavy dew of slumber.
Thou hast no figures nor no fantasies   250

255. **for your health:** healthy
257. **ungently:** discourteously
260. **across:** crossed
266. **wafture:** wave
269. **withal:** at the same time
270. **an effect of humor:** the result of a mood
271. **his:** i.e., its
274. **condition:** disposition
275. **know you Brutus:** i.e., **know you** to be **Brutus**
279. **come by it:** obtain it (his good **health**)

Portia.
From [Guillaume Rouillé,] . . . *Promptuarii iconum* . . . (1553).

Which busy care draws in the brains of men.
Therefore thou sleep'st so sound.

Enter Portia.

PORTIA   Brutus, my lord.
BRUTUS
Portia! What mean you? Wherefore rise you now?
It is not for your health thus to commit   255
Your weak condition to the raw cold morning.
PORTIA
Nor for yours neither. You've ungently, Brutus,
Stole from my bed. And yesternight at supper
You suddenly arose and walked about,
Musing and sighing, with your arms across,   260
And when I asked you what the matter was,
You stared upon me with ungentle looks.
I urged you further; then you scratched your head
And too impatiently stamped with your foot.
Yet I insisted; yet you answered not,   265
But with an angry wafture of your hand
Gave sign for me to leave you. So I did,
Fearing to strengthen that impatience
Which seemed too much enkindled, and withal
Hoping it was but an effect of humor,   270
Which sometime hath his hour with every man.
It will not let you eat nor talk nor sleep,
And could it work so much upon your shape
As it hath much prevailed on your condition,
I should not know you Brutus. Dear my lord,   275
Make me acquainted with your cause of grief.
BRUTUS
I am not well in health, and that is all.
PORTIA
Brutus is wise and, were he not in health,
He would embrace the means to come by it.

281. **physical:** good for one's health (i.e., in accord with the dictates of physic, or medicine)

282. **unbracèd:** See note to 1.3.51. **humors:** damp air

286. **rheumy:** dank, full of moisture; **unpurgèd:** i.e., not cleansed (by the sun's rays)

288. **sick offense:** harmful disorder

292. **charm:** conjure, entreat

293–94. **that great vow ... make us one:** "He that loveth his own wife loveth himself. ... For this cause shall a man ... be joined unto his wife, and they two shall be one flesh." "The Form of Solemnization of Matrimony," *The Book of Common Prayer ... in the Church of England*, 1559 (spelling modernized).

295. **unfold:** reveal

296. **heavy:** sad

303. **excepted:** made an exception that

305. **in sort or limitation:** only after a fashion or within limits

308. **suburbs:** outskirts (In Shakespeare's London, **the suburbs** were less regulated than the city, and were the location of brothels, theaters, and other buildings of bad repute.)

BRUTUS
Why so I do. Good Portia, go to bed.   280
PORTIA
Is Brutus sick? And is it physical
To walk unbracèd and suck up the humors
Of the dank morning? What, is Brutus sick,
And will he steal out of his wholesome bed
To dare the vile contagion of the night   285
And tempt the rheumy and unpurgèd air
To add unto ⌜his⌝ sickness? No, my Brutus,
You have some sick offense within your mind,
Which by the right and virtue of my place
I ought to know of. ⌜*She kneels.*⌝ And upon my   290
    knees
I charm you, by my once commended beauty,
By all your vows of love, and that great vow
Which did incorporate and make us one,
That you unfold to me, your self, your half,   295
Why you are heavy, and what men tonight
Have had resort to you; for here have been
Some six or seven who did hide their faces
Even from darkness.
BRUTUS   Kneel not, gentle Portia.   300
                              ⌜*He lifts her up.*⌝
PORTIA
I should not need, if you were gentle Brutus.
Within the bond of marriage, tell me, Brutus,
Is it excepted I should know no secrets
That appertain to you? Am I your self
But, as it were, in sort or limitation,   305
To keep with you at meals, comfort your bed,
And talk to you sometimes? Dwell I but in the
    suburbs
Of your good pleasure? If it be no more,
Portia is Brutus' harlot, not his wife.   310

315. **withal:** i.e., at the same time, even so

318. **Cato's daughter:** Marcus Porcius Cato, or Cato Uticensis, fought on Pompey's side and killed himself rather than be captured by Caesar. The Republicans considered him a martyr.

321. **counsels:** secrets

322. **constancy:** self-control, fortitude

324. **patience:** composure

329. **by and by:** soon

331. **engagements:** affairs in which I am engaged; **construe:** fully explain

332. **the charactery of:** that which is written on (i.e., the meaning of)

335. **sick man:** Lucius presumably interprets the **kerchief** (line 341) worn by Ligarius.

338. **how?:** i.e., **how** are you?

339. **Vouchsafe:** please accept

BRUTUS
You are my true and honorable wife,
As dear to me as are the ruddy drops
That visit my sad heart.

PORTIA
If this were true, then should I know this secret.
I grant I am a woman, but withal   315
A woman that Lord Brutus took to wife.
I grant I am a woman, but withal
A woman well-reputed, Cato's daughter.
Think you I am no stronger than my sex,
Being so fathered and so husbanded?   320
Tell me your counsels; I will not disclose 'em.
I have made strong proof of my constancy,
Giving myself a voluntary wound
Here, in the thigh. Can I bear that with patience,
And not my husband's secrets?   325

BRUTUS   O you gods,
Render me worthy of this noble wife!   *Knock.*
Hark, hark, one knocks. Portia, go in awhile,
And by and by thy bosom shall partake
The secrets of my heart.   330
All my engagements I will construe to thee,
All the charactery of my sad brows.
Leave me with haste.   *Portia exits.*
            Lucius, who 's that knocks?

Enter Lucius and Ligarius.

LUCIUS
Here is a sick man that would speak with you.   335

BRUTUS
Caius Ligarius, that Metellus spoke of.—
Boy, stand aside.   ⌜*Lucius exits.*⌝
            Caius Ligarius, how?

LIGARIUS
Vouchsafe good morrow from a feeble tongue.

341. **wear a kerchief:** In Shakespeare's England, men and women wrapped their heads in linen head-cloths when ill.

342. **have in hand:** has in process

351. **mortifièd spirit:** deadened vitality

357. **unfold:** reveal

359. **Set on your foot:** proceed

BRUTUS
O, what a time have you chose out, brave Caius,   340
To wear a kerchief! Would you were not sick!
LIGARIUS
I am not sick, if Brutus have in hand
Any exploit worthy the name of honor.
BRUTUS
Such an exploit have I in hand, Ligarius,
Had you a healthful ear to hear of it.   345
LIGARIUS
By all the gods that Romans bow before,
I here discard my sickness.
                  ⌜*He takes off his kerchief.*⌝
                  Soul of Rome,
Brave son derived from honorable loins,
Thou like an exorcist hast conjured up   350
My mortifièd spirit. Now bid me run,
And I will strive with things impossible,
Yea, get the better of them. What's to do?
BRUTUS
A piece of work that will make sick men whole.
LIGARIUS
But are not some whole that we must make sick?   355
BRUTUS
That must we also. What it is, my Caius,
I shall unfold to thee as we are going
To whom it must be done.
LIGARIUS   Set on your foot,
And with a heart new-fired I follow you   360
To do I know not what; but it sufficeth
That Brutus leads me on.   *Thunder.*
BRUTUS   Follow me then.
                         They exit.

2.2 It is now the fifteenth of March. Calphurnia, Caesar's wife, persuades him to stay home because she fears for his safety. Decius Brutus, arriving to accompany Caesar to the Capitol, convinces him that the senators plan to crown Caesar that day but that they may never renew their offer should they suspect he is afraid. Caesar changes his mind and decides to go. He is joined by Brutus and the rest of the conspirators, as well as by Mark Antony.

---

0 SD. **nightgown:** dressing gown
1. **Nor . . . nor:** neither . . . **nor**
5. **present:** immediate
6. **success:** good or bad outcomes
13. **stood on ceremonies:** believed in omens
16. **Recounts:** who **recounts**
20. **right form:** regular order

"Warriors fought upon the clouds." (2.2.19)
From Conrad Lycosthenes, *Prodigiorum* . . . (1557).

74

⌜Scene 2⌝

Thunder and lightning. Enter Julius Caesar in his
nightgown.

CAESAR
Nor heaven nor earth have been at peace tonight.
Thrice hath Calphurnia in her sleep cried out
"Help ho, they murder Caesar!"—Who's within?

Enter a Servant.

SERVANT My lord.
CAESAR
Go bid the priests do present sacrifice,   5
And bring me their opinions of success.
SERVANT I will, my lord.   *He exits.*

Enter Calphurnia.

CALPHURNIA
What mean you, Caesar? Think you to walk forth?
You shall not stir out of your house today.
CAESAR
Caesar shall forth. The things that threatened me   10
Ne'er looked but on my back. When they shall see
The face of Caesar, they are vanishèd.
CALPHURNIA
Caesar, I never stood on ceremonies,
Yet now they fright me. There is one within,
Besides the things that we have heard and seen,   15
Recounts most horrid sights seen by the watch.
A lioness hath whelpèd in the streets,
And graves have yawned and yielded up their dead.
Fierce fiery warriors ⌜fought⌝ upon the clouds
In ranks and squadrons and right form of war,   20
Which drizzled blood upon the Capitol.
The noise of battle hurtled in the air,
Horses ⌜did⌝ neigh, and dying men did groan,

25. **use:** that which is usual
29. **Yet:** i.e., despite all the omens
30. **Are to:** i.e., **are** as applicable **to**
42. **offering:** sacrificial animal (See picture, below.)
44. **in shame of:** i.e., to shame
53. **confidence:** overconfidence

Augurer reading the entrails of a bull. (2.2.42)
From Conrad Lycosthenes, *Prodigiorum* . . . (1557).

And ghosts did shriek and squeal about the streets.
O Caesar, these things are beyond all use,   25
And I do fear them.
CAESAR   What can be avoided
Whose end is purposed by the mighty gods?
Yet Caesar shall go forth, for these predictions
Are to the world in general as to Caesar.   30
CALPHURNIA
When beggars die there are no comets seen;
The heavens themselves blaze forth the death of
    princes.
CAESAR
Cowards die many times before their deaths;
The valiant never taste of death but once.   35
Of all the wonders that I yet have heard,
It seems to me most strange that men should fear,
Seeing that death, a necessary end,
Will come when it will come.

Enter a Servant.

                    What say the augurers?   40
SERVANT
They would not have you to stir forth today.
Plucking the entrails of an offering forth,
They could not find a heart within the beast.
CAESAR
The gods do this in shame of cowardice.
Caesar should be a beast without a heart   45
If he should stay at home today for fear.
No, Caesar shall not. Danger knows full well
That Caesar is more dangerous than he.
We ⌈are⌉ two lions littered in one day,
And I the elder and more terrible.   50
And Caesar shall go forth.
CALPHURNIA   Alas, my lord,
Your wisdom is consumed in confidence.

60. **humor:** mood, state of mind; whim

63. **Senate House:** Shakespeare seems to have the senators gather in the **Senate House** (perhaps the ancient *curia* located in the Roman Forum, or perhaps Pompey's Porch, a temporary location of Senate meetings, as in Plutarch's "Life of Julius Caesar") before moving on to the Capitol. The opening of Act 3, with Caesar and the senators walking through the streets of Rome (3.1.12) before entering the Capitol, would support this apparent separation of locations. (However, see 2.4.1 and 2.4.13, where the **Senate House** and the Capitol seem to be a single place.)

64. **in very happy time:** at a **very** good moment

80. **stays:** detains

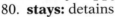

Statue of Julius Caesar.
From Giovanni Battista Cavalleriis,
Antiquarum statuarum . . . (1585–94).

Do not go forth today. Call it my fear
That keeps you in the house, and not your own.   55
We'll send Mark Antony to the Senate House,
And he shall say you are not well today.
Let me, upon my knee, prevail in this.   ⌜*She kneels.*⌝
CAESAR
Mark Antony shall say I am not well,
And for thy humor I will stay at home.   60
                    ⌜*He lifts her up.*⌝

Enter Decius.

Here's Decius Brutus; he shall tell them so.
DECIUS
Caesar, all hail! Good morrow, worthy Caesar.
I come to fetch you to the Senate House.
CAESAR
And you are come in very happy time
To bear my greeting to the Senators   65
And tell them that I will not come today.
Cannot is false, and that I dare not, falser.
I will not come today. Tell them so, Decius.
CALPHURNIA
Say he is sick.
CAESAR   Shall Caesar send a lie?   70
Have I in conquest stretched mine arm so far,
To be afeard to tell graybeards the truth?
Decius, go tell them Caesar will not come.
DECIUS
Most mighty Caesar, let me know some cause,
Lest I be laughed at when I tell them so.   75
CAESAR
The cause is in my will. I will not come.
That is enough to satisfy the Senate.
But for your private satisfaction,
Because I love you, I will let you know.
Calphurnia here, my wife, stays me at home.   80

81. **tonight:** i.e., last night

83. **lusty:** joyful, energetic

85. **for:** as; **portents:** accent on second syllable

93–94. **great men . . . cognizance:** Decius interprets Calphurnia's dream so that in it Caesar appears both as a religious martyr and as a great prince to whom **great men** press for tokens of favor. **tinctures, stains:** perhaps referring to the red **stains** on handkerchiefs dipped in the blood of martyrs or saints **relics:** remains of saints **cognizance:** a device identifying nobles of a royal house

101. **were:** would be

102. **Apt:** ready; **rendered:** made

108. **proceeding:** prospering, advancement

109. **reason . . . liable:** my sense of propriety is subordinate **to my love**

112. **robe:** perhaps, toga

She dreamt tonight she saw my statue,
Which, like a fountain with an hundred spouts,
Did run pure blood; and many lusty Romans
Came smiling and did bathe their hands in it.
And these does she apply for warnings and portents   85
And evils imminent, and on her knee
Hath begged that I will stay at home today.

DECIUS
This dream is all amiss interpreted.
It was a vision fair and fortunate.
Your statue spouting blood in many pipes,   90
In which so many smiling Romans bathed,
Signifies that from you great Rome shall suck
Reviving blood, and that great men shall press
For tinctures, stains, relics, and cognizance.
This by Calphurnia's dream is signified.   95

CAESAR
And this way have you well expounded it.

DECIUS
I have, when you have heard what I can say.
And know it now: the Senate have concluded
To give this day a crown to mighty Caesar.
If you shall send them word you will not come,   100
Their minds may change. Besides, it were a mock
Apt to be rendered, for someone to say
"Break up the Senate till another time,
When Caesar's wife shall meet with better dreams."
If Caesar hide himself, shall they not whisper   105
"Lo, Caesar is afraid"?
Pardon me, Caesar, for my dear dear love
To your proceeding bids me tell you this,
And reason to my love is liable.

CAESAR
How foolish do your fears seem now, Calphurnia!   110
I am ashamèd I did yield to them.
Give me my robe, for I will go.

118. **Caesar . . . enemy:** See 2.1.232–33.
119. **ague:** fever (pronounced ā-gue)
127. **to blame:** at fault
136. **every like is not the same:** Caesar had said, "we, **like** friends. . . ." Brutus responds with a version of the proverb "All that is alike **is not the same.**"
137. **earns:** grieves

Mark Antony.
From [Guillaume Rouillé,] . . . *Promptuarii iconum* . . . (1553).

Enter Brutus, Ligarius, Metellus, Casca, Trebonius,
Cinna, and Publius.

And look where Publius is come to fetch me.
PUBLIUS
Good morrow, Caesar.
CAESAR   Welcome, Publius.—   115
What, Brutus, are you stirred so early too?—
Good morrow, Casca.—Caius Ligarius,
Caesar was ne'er so much your enemy
As that same ague which hath made you lean.—
What is 't o'clock?   120
BRUTUS   Caesar, 'tis strucken eight.
CAESAR
I thank you for your pains and courtesy.

Enter Antony.

See, Antony that revels long a-nights
Is notwithstanding up.—Good morrow, Antony.
ANTONY   So to most noble Caesar.   125
CAESAR, ⌐*to Servant*¬   Bid them prepare within.—
I am to blame to be thus waited for.   ⌐*Servant exits.*¬
Now, Cinna.—Now, Metellus.—What, Trebonius,
I have an hour's talk in store for you.
Remember that you call on me today;   130
Be near me that I may remember you.
TREBONIUS
Caesar, I will. ⌐*Aside.*¬ And so near will I be
That your best friends shall wish I had been further.
CAESAR
Good friends, go in and taste some wine with me,
And we, like friends, will straightway go together.   135
BRUTUS, ⌐*aside*¬
That every like is not the same, O Caesar,
The heart of Brutus earns to think upon.
                                              They exit.

2.3 Artemidorus waits in the street for Caesar in order to give him a letter warning him of the conspiracy.

---

0 SD. **Artemidorus** of Cidnos was a teacher of rhetoric who was a friend of several of the conspirators and thus knew about the planned assassination.

7–8. **Security . . . to conspiracy:** overconfidence opens the way **to conspiracy**

9. **lover:** friend (i.e., one who loves you)

12. **suitor:** one who presents a petition

14. **Out of the teeth of emulation:** i.e., **out of** reach of envy

16. **Fates:** In classical mythology, the three **Fates** control a person's span of life, spinning, measuring, and finally cutting life's thread. (See picture, page 86.)

2.4 Portia, who has been told of the conspirators' plan to kill Caesar, waits anxiously for news of their success. She meets the Soothsayer, who still fears for Caesar and wants to warn him.

---

1. **Senate House:** See note to 2.2.63.

7. **constancy:** self-control, fortitude

9. **might:** strength

⌜Scene 3⌝

Enter Artemidorus ⌜reading a paper.⌝

ARTEMIDORUS *Caesar, beware of Brutus, take heed of*
Cassius, come not near Casca, have an eye to Cinna,
trust not Trebonius, mark well Metellus Cimber.
Decius Brutus loves thee not. Thou hast wronged
Caius Ligarius. There is but one mind in all these 5
men, and it is bent against Caesar. If thou beest not
immortal, look about you. Security gives way to
conspiracy. The mighty gods defend thee!
> *Thy lover,*
> *Artemidorus* 10

Here will I stand till Caesar pass along,
And as a suitor will I give him this.
My heart laments that virtue cannot live
Out of the teeth of emulation.
If thou read this, O Caesar, thou mayest live; 15
If not, the Fates with traitors do contrive.　*He exits.*

⌜Scene 4⌝

Enter Portia and Lucius.

PORTIA
I prithee, boy, run to the Senate House.
Stay not to answer me, but get thee gone.
Why dost thou stay?
LUCIUS　　　　　　To know my errand, madam.
PORTIA
I would have had thee there and here again 5
Ere I can tell thee what thou shouldst do there.
⌜*Aside.*⌝ O constancy, be strong upon my side;
Set a huge mountain 'tween my heart and tongue.
I have a man's mind but a woman's might.

10. **to keep counsel:** to observe secrecy (Proverbial: "**Women** can **keep** no **counsel**.")

11. **here yet:** still **here**

17. **suitors:** petitioners

21. **rumor:** noise

23. **Sooth:** i.e., in truth

23 SD. **Soothsayer:** the same prophet who, at 1.2.21 and 28, warned Caesar to "beware the ides of March"

The Fates. (2.3.16; 3.1.109)
From Vincenzo Cartari, *Imagines deorum* . . . (1581).

How hard it is for women to keep counsel!—   10
Art thou here yet?
LUCIUS   Madam, what should I do?
Run to the Capitol, and nothing else?
And so return to you, and nothing else?
PORTIA
Yes, bring me word, boy, if thy lord look well,   15
For he went sickly forth. And take good note
What Caesar doth, what suitors press to him.
Hark, boy, what noise is that?
LUCIUS I hear none, madam.
PORTIA Prithee, listen well.   20
I heard a bustling rumor like a fray,
And the wind brings it from the Capitol.
LUCIUS Sooth, madam, I hear nothing.

Enter the Soothsayer.

PORTIA
Come hither, fellow. Which way hast thou been?
SOOTHSAYER At mine own house, good lady.   25
PORTIA What is 't o'clock?
SOOTHSAYER About the ninth hour, lady.
PORTIA
Is Caesar yet gone to the Capitol?
SOOTHSAYER
Madam, not yet. I go to take my stand
To see him pass on to the Capitol.   30
PORTIA
Thou hast some suit to Caesar, hast thou not?
SOOTHSAYER
That I have, lady. If it will please Caesar
To be so good to Caesar as to hear me,
I shall beseech him to befriend himself.
PORTIA
Why, know'st thou any harms intended towards   35
    him?

38. **chance:** happen
41. **praetors:** judges
43. **more void:** less crowded
47. **speed:** prosper
52. **commend me:** i.e., convey my good wishes
53. **merry:** in good spirits

SOOTHSAYER
   None that I know will be, much that I fear may
      chance.
   Good morrow to you.—Here the street is narrow.
   The throng that follows Caesar at the heels,   40
   Of senators, of praetors, common suitors,
   Will crowd a feeble man almost to death.
   I'll get me to a place more void, and there
   Speak to great Caesar as he comes along.   *He exits.*
PORTIA
   I must go in. ⌜*Aside.*⌝ Ay me, how weak a thing   45
   The heart of woman is! O Brutus,
   The heavens speed thee in thine enterprise!
   Sure the boy heard me. ⌜*To Lucius.*⌝ Brutus hath a
      suit
   That Caesar will not grant. ⌜*Aside.*⌝ O, I grow   50
      faint.—
   Run, Lucius, and commend me to my lord.
   Say I am merry. Come to me again
   And bring me word what he doth say to thee.
                              They exit ⌜separately.⌝

The Tragedy of

JULIUS CAESAR

ACT 3

3.1   In the street Caesar brushes aside Artemidorus's attempt to warn him of the conspiracy. Once inside the Capitol, the conspirators gather around Caesar under the guise of pleading for the return of an exile. Beginning with Casca they stab Caesar to death and bathe their arms and hands in his blood. Ignoring Cassius's advice, Brutus gives Antony permission to speak at Caesar's funeral. Pretending to support Brutus, Antony plans to use this opportunity to turn the Roman people against the conspirators.

---

0 SD. **Flourish:** a trumpet or cornetto fanfare announcing a ceremonial entrance or exit

3. **schedule:** document

7. **touches . . . nearer:** more closely concerns **Caesar**

8. **us ourself:** This "royal plural" is normally used by kings.

11. **Sirrah:** a term of address to a male of inferior social status

13 SD. The action is to be imagined as shifting from **the street** (line 12) into **the Capitol**. Historical accounts place Caesar's death in a room off Pompey's Porch, but Shakespeare follows a tradition that places it in **the Capitol**. (See also *Hamlet* 3.2.109–10.)

ACT 3

⌐Scene 1¬

Flourish. Enter Caesar, Antony, Lepidus; Brutus, Cassius,
Casca, Decius, Metellus, Trebonius, Cinna; Publius,
⌐Popilius,¬Artemidorus, the Soothsayer, ⌐and other
Senators and Petitioners.¬

CAESAR The ides of March are come.
SOOTHSAYER Ay, Caesar, but not gone.
ARTEMIDORUS Hail, Caesar. Read this schedule.
DECIUS
Trebonius doth desire you to o'erread,
At your best leisure, this his humble suit.   5
ARTEMIDORUS
O Caesar, read mine first, for mine's a suit
That touches Caesar nearer. Read it, great Caesar.
CAESAR
What touches us ourself shall be last served.
ARTEMIDORUS
Delay not, Caesar; read it instantly.
CAESAR
What, is the fellow mad?   10
PUBLIUS   Sirrah, give place.
CASSIUS
What, urge you your petitions in the street?
Come to the Capitol.
                    ⌐Caesar goes forward, the rest following.¬

93

19. **is discoverèd:** has been revealed

20. **makes to:** approaches; **Mark:** i.e., look at, observe

21. **sudden:** swift; **prevention:** being forestalled

23. **Cassius . . . turn back:** i.e., neither **Cassius** nor **Caesar** will return home alive

25. **constant:** steady, calm

27. **Caesar:** i.e., Caesar's face

28. **look you:** i.e., **look**

31. **presently prefer his suit:** immediately present his petition

32. **addressed:** ready (to act)

33. **are . . . rears:** i.e., will be **the first** to raise

36. **puissant:** powerful

Julius Caesar.
From [Guillaume Rouillé,] . . . *Promptuarii iconum* . . . (1553).

POPILIUS, ⌜*to Cassius*⌝
  I wish your enterprise today may thrive.
CASSIUS What enterprise, Popilius?   15
POPILIUS Fare you well.   ⌜*He walks away.*⌝
BRUTUS What said Popilius Lena?
CASSIUS
  He wished today our enterprise might thrive.
  I fear our purpose is discoverèd.
BRUTUS
  Look how he makes to Caesar. Mark him.   20
CASSIUS
  Casca, be sudden, for we fear prevention.—
  Brutus, what shall be done? If this be known,
  Cassius or Caesar never shall turn back,
  For I will slay myself.
BRUTUS   Cassius, be constant.   25
  Popilius Lena speaks not of our purposes,
  For look, he smiles, and Caesar doth not change.
CASSIUS
  Trebonius knows his time, for look you, Brutus,
  He draws Mark Antony out of the way.
                    ⌜*Trebonius and Antony exit.*⌝
DECIUS
  Where is Metellus Cimber? Let him go   30
  And presently prefer his suit to Caesar.
BRUTUS
  He is addressed. Press near and second him.
CINNA
  Casca, you are the first that rears your hand.
CAESAR
  Are we all ready? What is now amiss
  That Caesar and his Senate must redress?   35
METELLUS, ⌜*kneeling*⌝
  Most high, most mighty, and most puissant Caesar,
  Metellus Cimber throws before thy seat
  An humble heart.

39. **prevent:** forestall

40. **couchings and . . . lowly courtesies:** low bows and curtsies

41. **fire the blood:** In the metaphor Caesar begins here, heated **blood** is presented as rebellious against reason (**rebel blood**, line 44) and susceptible to flattery, while reason and self-control are linked to coldness and constancy, to **blood** that refuses to **be thawed** (line 45) or melted (line 46).

42. **preordinance and first decree:** earlier judicial decisions already proclaimed

43. **the law of children:** i.e., rules in a children's game; **fond:** foolish

51. **spurn:** kick

52. **doth not wrong:** does not act unjustly

53. **satisfied:** i.e., content to grant the pardon

64. **well moved:** (1) easily swayed; (2) strongly affected

65. **pray to move:** beg others (i.e., as you are doing) to change

66. **constant as the Northern Star:** immovable as the polestar

67. **resting:** stationary

68. **fellow:** equal

69. **unnumbered:** innumerable

CAESAR   I must prevent thee, Cimber.
These couchings and these lowly courtesies   40
Might fire the blood of ordinary men
And turn preordinance and first decree
Into the ⌐law⌐ of children. Be not fond
To think that Caesar bears such rebel blood
That will be thawed from the true quality   45
With that which melteth fools—I mean sweet
    words,
Low-crookèd curtsies, and base spaniel fawning.
Thy brother by decree is banishèd.
If thou dost bend and pray and fawn for him,   50
I spurn thee like a cur out of my way.
Know: Caesar doth not wrong, nor without cause
Will he be satisfied.
METELLUS
Is there no voice more worthy than my own
To sound more sweetly in great Caesar's ear   55
For the repealing of my banished brother?
BRUTUS, ⌐*kneeling*⌐
I kiss thy hand, but not in flattery, Caesar,
Desiring thee that Publius Cimber may
Have an immediate freedom of repeal.
CAESAR
What, Brutus?   60
CASSIUS, ⌐*kneeling*⌐
           Pardon, Caesar; Caesar, pardon!
As low as to thy foot doth Cassius fall
To beg enfranchisement for Publius Cimber.
CAESAR
I could be well moved, if I were as you.
If I could pray to move, prayers would move me.   65
But I am constant as the Northern Star,
Of whose true fixed and resting quality
There is no fellow in the firmament.
The skies are painted with unnumbered sparks;

71. **doth . . . place:** keeps its (fixed) position

73. **apprehensive:** able to apprehend

76. **Unshaked of motion:** (1) unmoved by petition; (2) unaffected by inner agitation

78. **constant:** resolute

81. **lift up Olympus:** i.e., try to do the impossible (Olympus is a mountain in Greece so high it was thought to be the home of the gods.)

83. **Brutus:** i.e., even **Brutus; bootless:** uselessly

85. **Et tu, Brutè?:** i.e., you also, Brutus? (Latin)

88. **common pulpits:** platforms used for public speeches

94. **Publius:** an old senator, stunned (**confounded** [line 95]) by what has happened

95. **mutiny:** uproar

Assassination of Caesar and ascent of his spirit. (3.1.85 SD)
From Ovid, *Metamorphoses* . . . (1591).

They are all fire, and every one doth shine.   70
But there's but one in all doth hold his place.
So in the world: 'tis furnished well with men,
And men are flesh and blood, and apprehensive.
Yet in the number I do know but one
That unassailable holds on his rank,   75
Unshaked of motion; and that I am he
Let me a little show it, even in this:
That I was constant Cimber should be banished
And constant do remain to keep him so.
CINNA, ⌜*kneeling*⌝
  O Caesar—   80
CAESAR   Hence. Wilt thou lift up Olympus?
DECIUS, ⌜*kneeling*⌝
  Great Caesar—
CAESAR   Doth not Brutus bootless kneel?
CASCA   Speak, hands, for me!
    ⌜*As Casca strikes, the others rise up and*⌝ *stab Caesar.*
CAESAR   *Et tu, Brutè?*—Then fall, Caesar.   85
                          ⌜*He*⌝ *dies.*
CINNA
  Liberty! Freedom! Tyranny is dead!
  Run hence, proclaim, cry it about the streets.
CASSIUS
  Some to the common pulpits and cry out
  "Liberty, freedom, and enfranchisement."
BRUTUS
  People and Senators, be not affrighted.   90
  Fly not; stand still. Ambition's debt is paid.
CASCA
  Go to the pulpit, Brutus.
DECIUS   And Cassius too.
BRUTUS   Where's Publius?
CINNA
  Here, quite confounded with this mutiny.   95

98. **of standing:** i.e., of having to **stand fast** (line 96)

102. **your age:** you as an old man; **mischief:** injury

103. **abide:** stay; face the consequences of

106. **amazed:** stunned

108. **doomsday:** in Christian thought, the day on which the dead will be raised, judged, and sent either to heaven or hell (See picture, below.)

109. **Fates:** See note to 2.3.16.

112. **drawing days out:** prolonging life; **stand upon:** i.e., care about

Doomsday. (3.1.107–8)
From Thomas Fisher's etching of the wall painting of Doomsday in the Guild Chapel at Stratford-upon-Avon (1807).

METELLUS
  Stand fast together, lest some friend of Caesar's
  Should chance—
BRUTUS
  Talk not of standing.—Publius, good cheer.
  There is no harm intended to your person,
  Nor to no Roman else. So tell them, Publius.   100
CASSIUS
  And leave us, Publius, lest that the people,
  Rushing on us, should do your age some mischief.
BRUTUS
  Do so, and let no man abide this deed
  But we the doers.
                    ⌜*All but the Conspirators exit.*⌝

              Enter Trebonius.

CASSIUS Where is Antony?   105
TREBONIUS Fled to his house amazed.
  Men, wives, and children stare, cry out, and run
  As it were doomsday.
BRUTUS   Fates, we will know your
    pleasures.   110
  That we shall die we know; 'tis but the time,
  And drawing days out, that men stand upon.
CASCA
  Why, he that cuts off twenty years of life
  Cuts off so many years of fearing death.
BRUTUS
  Grant that, and then is death a benefit.   115
  So are we Caesar's friends, that have abridged
  His time of fearing death. Stoop, Romans, stoop,
  And let us bathe our hands in Caesar's blood
  Up to the elbows and besmear our swords.
  Then walk we forth, even to the marketplace,   120
  And, waving our red weapons o'er our heads,
  Let's all cry "Peace, freedom, and liberty!"

127. **in sport:** in performances of plays

128. **Pompey's basis:** the base of **Pompey's** statue; **along:** prostrate

137. **Soft:** i.e., wait a minute

145. **vouchsafe:** allow

146. **resolved:** (satisfactorily) answered, brought to a clear understanding

CASSIUS
    Stoop then, and wash.
⌐*They smear their hands and swords with Caesar's blood.*⌐
                        How many ages hence
    Shall this our lofty scene be acted over   125
    In ⌐states⌐ unborn and accents yet unknown!
BRUTUS
    How many times shall Caesar bleed in sport,
    That now on Pompey's basis ⌐lies⌐ along
    No worthier than the dust!
CASSIUS   So oft as that shall be,   130
    So often shall the knot of us be called
    The men that gave their country liberty.
DECIUS
    What, shall we forth?
CASSIUS   Ay, every man away.
    Brutus shall lead, and we will grace his heels   135
    With the most boldest and best hearts of Rome.

                    Enter a Servant.

BRUTUS
    Soft, who comes here? A friend of Antony's.
SERVANT, ⌐*kneeling*⌐
    Thus, Brutus, did my master bid me kneel.
    Thus did Mark Antony bid me fall down,
    And, being prostrate, thus he bade me say: 140
    Brutus is noble, wise, valiant, and honest;
    Caesar was mighty, bold, royal, and loving.
    Say, I love Brutus, and I honor him;
    Say, I feared Caesar, honored him, and loved him.
    If Brutus will vouchsafe that Antony   145
    May safely come to him and be resolved
    How Caesar hath deserved to lie in death,
    Mark Antony shall not love Caesar dead
    So well as Brutus living, but will follow
    The fortunes and affairs of noble Brutus   150

151. **Thorough:** through; **untrod:** i.e., unprecedented (literally, untraversed)

155. **so please him come:** i.e., if it pleases him to **come**

159. **to friend:** i.e., as our **friend**

161. **still:** always

162. **shrewdly to the purpose:** uncomfortably close to the truth

168. **let blood:** i.e., killed (literally, bled); **rank:** corrupt, with the second sense of "grown too large," and thus in need of cutting (either to release diseased blood or to reduce in size)

173. **bear me hard:** hold a grudge against me

174. **purpled:** crimsoned

175. **Live:** i.e., if I **live**

176. **apt:** ready

177. **mean:** means, way or method

Thorough the hazards of this untrod state
With all true faith. So says my master Antony.
BRUTUS
Thy master is a wise and valiant Roman.
I never thought him worse.
Tell him, so please him come unto this place,   155
He shall be satisfied and, by my honor,
Depart untouched.
SERVANT   I'll fetch him presently.
                                        Servant exits.
BRUTUS
I know that we shall have him well to friend.
CASSIUS
I wish we may; but yet have I a mind   160
That fears him much, and my misgiving still
Falls shrewdly to the purpose.

                    Enter Antony.

BRUTUS
But here comes Antony.—Welcome, Mark Antony!
ANTONY
O mighty Caesar, dost thou lie so low?
Are all thy conquests, glories, triumphs, spoils   165
Shrunk to this little measure? Fare thee well.—
I know not, gentlemen, what you intend,
Who else must be let blood, who else is rank.
If I myself, there is no hour so fit
As Caesar's death's hour, nor no instrument   170
Of half that worth as those your swords made rich
With the most noble blood of all this world.
I do beseech you, if you bear me hard,
Now, whilst your purpled hands do reek and smoke,
Fulfill your pleasure. Live a thousand years,   175
I shall not find myself so apt to die;
No place will please me so, no mean of death,

178. **cut off:** put to death
181. **bloody:** (1) bloodthirsty; (2) covered with blood
185. **pitiful:** i.e., filled with pity
187. **so pity pity:** i.e., **so pity drives out pity**
189. **leaden:** made of lead, and therefore blunt
190–91. **Our arms . . . brothers' temper:** i.e., both **our** bloody **arms** and **our** loving **hearts   in strength of malice:** seeming strong in enmity   **of brothers' temper:** full of brotherly feeling
194. **disposing:** bestowing; **dignities:** offices of state
197. **deliver you:** declare to you, tell you
200. **doubt not of:** do **not doubt**
210. **credit:** credibility
211. **conceit:** regard

As here by Caesar, and by you cut off,
The choice and master spirits of this age.
BRUTUS
  O Antony, beg not your death of us!   180
  Though now we must appear bloody and cruel,
  As by our hands and this our present act
  You see we do, yet see you but our hands
  And this the bleeding business they have done.
  Our hearts you see not; they are pitiful;   185
  And pity to the general wrong of Rome
  (As fire drives out fire, so pity pity)
  Hath done this deed on Caesar. For your part,
  To you our swords have leaden points, Mark Antony.
  Our arms in strength of malice, and our hearts   190
  Of brothers' temper, do receive you in
  With all kind love, good thoughts, and reverence.
CASSIUS
  Your voice shall be as strong as any man's
  In the disposing of new dignities.
BRUTUS
  Only be patient till we have appeased   195
  The multitude, beside themselves with fear;
  And then we will deliver you the cause
  Why I, that did love Caesar when I struck him,
  Have thus proceeded.
ANTONY   I doubt not of your wisdom.   200
  Let each man render me his bloody hand.
  First, Marcus Brutus, will I shake with you.—
  Next, Caius Cassius, do I take your hand.—
  Now, Decius Brutus, yours;—now yours,
    Metellus;—   205
  Yours, Cinna;—and, my valiant Casca, yours;—
  Though last, not least in love, yours, good
    Trebonius.—
  Gentlemen all—alas, what shall I say?
  My credit now stands on such slippery ground   210
  That one of two bad ways you must conceit me,

215. **dearer:** more keenly

221. **close:** join, unite

223. **bayed:** brought to bay (the position of an animal cornered by pursuers); cornered

224. **hart:** stag (with a pun on "heart") See picture, page 110.

226. **Signed . . . spoil:** marked with the signs of your destruction; **Lethe:** i.e., death (literally, the river of oblivion in Hades) Shakespeare may have been influenced by the Latin word *letum*—often spelled *lethum*—which means "death."

228. **the heart of thee:** thy **heart**

234. **cold modesty:** unimpassioned moderation

236. **compact:** accent on second syllable

237. **pricked:** i.e., counted

238. **shall we on: shall we** proceed

239. **Therefore:** i.e., it was in answer to that question that

244. **Or else were this:** otherwise this would be

Either a coward or a flatterer.—
That I did love thee, Caesar, O, 'tis true!
If then thy spirit look upon us now,
Shall it not grieve thee dearer than thy death   215
To see thy Antony making his peace,
Shaking the bloody fingers of thy foes—
Most noble!—in the presence of thy corpse?
Had I as many eyes as thou hast wounds,
Weeping as fast as they stream forth thy blood,   220
It would become me better than to close
In terms of friendship with thine enemies.
Pardon me, Julius! Here wast thou bayed, brave
    hart,
Here didst thou fall, and here thy hunters stand   225
Signed in thy spoil and crimsoned in thy Lethe.
O world, thou wast the forest to this hart,
And this indeed, O world, the heart of thee.
How like a deer strucken by many princes
Dost thou here lie!   230
CASSIUS   Mark Antony—
ANTONY   Pardon me, Caius Cassius.
The enemies of Caesar shall say this;
Then, in a friend, it is cold modesty.
CASSIUS
I blame you not for praising Caesar so.   235
But what compact mean you to have with us?
Will you be pricked in number of our friends,
Or shall we on and not depend on you?
ANTONY
Therefore I took your hands, but was indeed
Swayed from the point by looking down on Caesar.   240
Friends am I with you all and love you all,
Upon this hope, that you shall give me reasons
Why and wherein Caesar was dangerous.
BRUTUS
Or else were this a savage spectacle.

250. **Produce:** bring forward (Latin *producere*)
251. **in the pulpit:** on the public platform
252. **in the order . . . funeral: in the** course **of his** funeral ceremonies
261. **will myself:** i.e., **will** go **myself**
263. **What Antony shall:** whatever **Antony** may; **protest:** proclaim
267. **advantage:** benefit (us)
268. **fall:** befall, happen

Hart at bay. (3.1.223–24)
From George Turberville, *The noble art of venerie* . . . (1611).

Our reasons are so full of good regard   245
That were you, Antony, the son of Caesar,
You should be satisfied.
ANTONY   That's all I seek;
And am, moreover, suitor that I may
Produce his body to the marketplace,   250
And in the pulpit, as becomes a friend,
Speak in the order of his funeral.
BRUTUS
 You shall, Mark Antony.
CASSIUS   Brutus, a word with you.
 ⌜*Aside to Brutus.*⌝ You know not what you do. Do 255
  not consent
That Antony speak in his funeral.
Know you how much the people may be moved
By that which he will utter?
BRUTUS, ⌜*aside to Cassius*⌝ By your pardon, 260
I will myself into the pulpit first
And show the reason of our Caesar's death.
What Antony shall speak I will protest
He speaks by leave and by permission,
And that we are contented Caesar shall   265
Have all true rites and lawful ceremonies.
It shall advantage more than do us wrong.
CASSIUS, ⌜*aside to Brutus*⌝
I know not what may fall. I like it not.
BRUTUS
Mark Antony, here, take you Caesar's body.
You shall not in your funeral speech blame us 270
But speak all good you can devise of Caesar
And say you do 't by our permission,
Else shall you not have any hand at all
About his funeral. And you shall speak
In the same pulpit whereto I am going,   275
After my speech is ended.

283. **tide of times:** current or flow of history
286. **dumb:** mute, silent
289. **Domestic:** synonymous with **civil**
290. **cumber:** overwhelm
291. **in use:** customary
292. **objects:** sights
294. **quartered:** cut in four pieces
295. **fell:** fatal; cruel
296. **ranging:** roaming like an animal seeking prey
297. **Ate:** goddess of discord and vengeance (pronounced as two syllables)
299. **"Havoc!":** the war cry that meant "give no quarter" (i.e., seize or slaughter at will); **let slip:** unleash
301. **carrion:** rotting

ANTONY   Be it so.
  I do desire no more.
BRUTUS
  Prepare the body, then, and follow us.
                                    All but Antony exit.
ANTONY
  O pardon me, thou bleeding piece of earth,   280
  That I am meek and gentle with these butchers.
  Thou art the ruins of the noblest man
  That ever livèd in the tide of times.
  Woe to the hand that shed this costly blood!
  Over thy wounds now do I prophesy   285
  (Which like dumb mouths do ope their ruby lips
  To beg the voice and utterance of my tongue)
  A curse shall light upon the limbs of men;
  Domestic fury and fierce civil strife
  Shall cumber all the parts of Italy;   290
  Blood and destruction shall be so in use
  And dreadful objects so familiar
  That mothers shall but smile when they behold
  Their infants quartered with the hands of war,
  All pity choked with custom of fell deeds;   295
  And Caesar's spirit, ranging for revenge,
  With Ate by his side come hot from hell,
  Shall in these confines with a monarch's voice
  Cry "Havoc!" and let slip the dogs of war,
  That this foul deed shall smell above the earth   300
  With carrion men groaning for burial.

                Enter Octavius' Servant.

  You serve Octavius Caesar, do you not?
SERVANT   I do, Mark Antony.
ANTONY
  Caesar did write for him to come to Rome.
SERVANT
  He did receive his letters and is coming,   305

308. **big:** full (of grief)
309. **Passion:** emotion
313. **Post:** ride quickly
317. **Hie:** go
319. **try:** test, attempt to discover
321. **issue of:** result produced by; **bloody:** See note to 3.1.181, above.

3.2 Brutus explains to the people that the cause of Caesar's assassination was the preservation of the Roman Republic from Caesar's ambition to be king. Mark Antony, bringing in Caesar's body, refutes Brutus's charge of ambition against Caesar, displays Caesar's wounds, and reveals that Caesar had made the common people his heirs. Inflamed by Antony's words, the people set off to attack the conspirators. A servant then informs Antony that Octavius Caesar, Antony's ally, has come to Rome and that Brutus and Cassius have been forced to flee.

---

0 SD. **Plebeians:** commoners
4. **part the numbers:** divide those gathered

And bid me say to you by word of mouth—
O Caesar!

ANTONY
Thy heart is big. Get thee apart and weep.
Passion, I see, is catching, ⌜for⌝ mine eyes,
Seeing those beads of sorrow stand in thine,   310
Began to water. Is thy master coming?

SERVANT
He lies tonight within seven leagues of Rome.

ANTONY
Post back with speed and tell him what hath
    chanced.
Here is a mourning Rome, a dangerous Rome,   315
No Rome of safety for Octavius yet.
Hie hence and tell him so.—Yet stay awhile;
Thou shalt not back till I have borne this corpse
Into the marketplace. There shall I try,
In my oration, how the people take   320
The cruel issue of these bloody men,
According to the which thou shalt discourse
To young Octavius of the state of things.
Lend me your hand.
                    They exit ⌜with Caesar's body.⌝

⌜Scene 2⌝

Enter Brutus and Cassius with the Plebeians.

⌜PLEBEIANS⌝
We will be satisfied! Let us be satisfied!

BRUTUS
Then follow me and give me audience, friends.—
Cassius, go you into the other street
And part the numbers.—
Those that will hear me speak, let 'em stay here;   5
Those that will follow Cassius, go with him;

11. **severally:** separately
11 SD. **pulpit:** See note to 3.1.88.
14. **lovers:** friends
17. **Censure:** judge
28. **ambitious:** greedy for power
30. **ambition:** inordinate desire for high rank or influence (See picture of a personified **Ambition**, below.)
31. **bondman:** bond servant, slave
32. **rude:** uncivilized

Ambition. (3.2.28, 30, 106)
From Cesare Ripa, *Iconologia* . . . (1610).

And public reasons shall be renderèd
Of Caesar's death.
FIRST PLEBEIAN   I will hear Brutus speak.
SECOND PLEBEIAN
I will hear Cassius, and compare their reasons   10
When severally we hear them renderèd.
                    ⌜*Cassius exits with some of the Plebeians.*
                    Brutus goes into the pulpit.⌝
THIRD PLEBEIAN
The noble Brutus is ascended. Silence.
BRUTUS Be patient till the last.
Romans, countrymen, and lovers, hear me for my
cause, and be silent that you may hear. Believe me   15
for mine honor, and have respect to mine honor
that you may believe. Censure me in your wisdom,
and awake your senses that you may the better
judge. If there be any in this assembly, any dear
friend of Caesar's, to him I say that Brutus' love   20
to Caesar was no less than his. If then that friend
demand why Brutus rose against Caesar, this is my
answer: not that I loved Caesar less, but that I loved
Rome more. Had you rather Caesar were living, and
die all slaves, than that Caesar were dead, to live all   25
freemen? As Caesar loved me, I weep for him. As he
was fortunate, I rejoice at it. As he was valiant, I
honor him. But, as he was ambitious, I slew him.
There is tears for his love, joy for his fortune, honor
for his valor, and death for his ambition. Who is   30
here so base that would be a bondman? If any,
speak, for him have I offended. Who is here so rude
that would not be a Roman? If any, speak, for him
have I offended. Who is here so vile that will not
love his country? If any, speak, for him have I   35
offended. I pause for a reply.
PLEBEIANS None, Brutus, none.
BRUTUS Then none have I offended. I have done no

39. **you shall . . . Brutus:** i.e., you will be allowed to **do to Brutus** if he offends in the same way

39–40. **The question . . . is enrolled:** the considerations that led to **his death** are written on a scroll

41. **extenuated:** minimized

42. **enforced:** emphasized

45–46. **a place in the commonwealth:** citizenship in a free state

47. **lover:** friend

63. **Do grace to:** honor; **grace his speech:** i.e., be gracious to, show favor to, Antony's public address

more to Caesar than you shall do to Brutus. The
question of his death is enrolled in the Capitol, his   40
glory not extenuated wherein he was worthy, nor
his offenses enforced for which he suffered death.

Enter Mark Antony ⌐and others⌐ with Caesar's body.

Here comes his body, mourned by Mark Antony,
who, though he had no hand in his death, shall
receive the benefit of his dying—a place in the   45
commonwealth—as which of you shall not? With
this I depart: that, as I slew my best lover for the
good of Rome, I have the same dagger for myself
when it shall please my country to need my death.

PLEBEIANS   Live, Brutus, live, live!   50

FIRST PLEBEIAN
Bring him with triumph home unto his house.

SECOND PLEBEIAN
Give him a statue with his ancestors.

THIRD PLEBEIAN
Let him be Caesar.

FOURTH PLEBEIAN   Caesar's better parts
Shall be crowned in Brutus.   55

FIRST PLEBEIAN
We'll bring him to his house with shouts and
   clamors.

BRUTUS
My countrymen—

SECOND PLEBEIAN   Peace, silence! Brutus speaks.

FIRST PLEBEIAN   Peace, ho!   60

BRUTUS
Good countrymen, let me depart alone,
And, for my sake, stay here with Antony.
Do grace to Caesar's corpse, and grace his speech
Tending to Caesar's glories, which Mark Antony
(By our permission) is allowed to make.   65

69. **public chair:** the rostrum from which Brutus had been speaking

80. **gentle:** a complimentary epithet

87. **ambitious:** See note to 3.2.28.

88. **grievous:** terrible

89. **grievously:** at a heavy rate or high price; **answered:** paid for

90. **under leave of:** with the permission of

Funeral oration.
From Tommaso Porcacchi, *Funerali antichi* . . . (1591).

I do entreat you, not a man depart,
Save I alone, till Antony have spoke.
                    He ⌐descends and ⌐exits.
FIRST PLEBEIAN
Stay, ho, and let us hear Mark Antony!
THIRD PLEBEIAN
Let him go up into the public chair.
⌐PLEBEIANS⌐
We'll hear him.—Noble Antony, go up.   70
ANTONY
For Brutus' sake, I am beholding to you.
                    ⌐He goes into the pulpit.⌐
FOURTH PLEBEIAN   What does he say of Brutus?
THIRD PLEBEIAN   He says for Brutus' sake
He finds himself beholding to us all.
FOURTH PLEBEIAN
'Twere best he speak no harm of Brutus here.   75
FIRST PLEBEIAN
This Caesar was a tyrant.
THIRD PLEBEIAN   Nay, that's certain.
We are blest that Rome is rid of him.
SECOND PLEBEIAN
Peace, let us hear what Antony can say.
ANTONY
You gentle Romans—   80
PLEBEIANS   Peace, ho! Let us hear him.
ANTONY
Friends, Romans, countrymen, lend me your ears.
I come to bury Caesar, not to praise him.
The evil that men do lives after them;
The good is oft interrèd with their bones.   85
So let it be with Caesar. The noble Brutus
Hath told you Caesar was ambitious.
If it were so, it was a grievous fault,
And grievously hath Caesar answered it.
Here, under leave of Brutus and the rest   90
(For Brutus is an honorable man;

97. **He:** i.e., Caesar
104. **the Lupercal: the** day of the feast of **Lupercal**
106. **ambition:** See note to 3.2.30.

"He hath brought many captives home to Rome." (3.2.97)
From Onofrio Panvinio, *De lvdis circensibvs, libri II.*
De trivmphis liber vnvs . . . (1642).

So are they all, all honorable men),
Come I to speak in Caesar's funeral.
He was my friend, faithful and just to me,
But Brutus says he was ambitious,   95
And Brutus is an honorable man.
He hath brought many captives home to Rome,
Whose ransoms did the general coffers fill.
Did this in Caesar seem ambitious?
When that the poor have cried, Caesar hath wept;   100
Ambition should be made of sterner stuff.
Yet Brutus says he was ambitious,
And Brutus is an honorable man.
You all did see that on the Lupercal
I thrice presented him a kingly crown,   105
Which he did thrice refuse. Was this ambition?
Yet Brutus says he was ambitious,
And sure he is an honorable man.
I speak not to disprove what Brutus spoke,
But here I am to speak what I do know.   110
You all did love him once, not without cause.
What cause withholds you, then, to mourn for
    him?—
O judgment, thou ⌜art⌝ fled to brutish beasts,
And men have lost their reason!—Bear with me;   115
My heart is in the coffin there with Caesar,
And I must pause till it come back to me. ⌜*He weeps.*⌝
FIRST PLEBEIAN
Methinks there is much reason in his sayings.
SECOND PLEBEIAN
If thou consider rightly of the matter,
Caesar has had great wrong.   120
THIRD PLEBEIAN   Has he, masters?
I fear there will a worse come in his place.
FOURTH PLEBEIAN
Marked you his words? He would not take the
    crown;
Therefore 'tis certain he was not ambitious.   125

126. **dear abide it:** pay for it dearly
129. **mark:** i.e., listen to
132. **none . . . reverence:** i.e., no one is so insignificant as to be his inferior, owing him deference
141. **closet:** private room
142. **commons:** people
145. **napkins:** handkerchiefs
146. **memory:** i.e., a memento
149. **issue:** heirs

FIRST PLEBEIAN
If it be found so, some will dear abide it.
SECOND PLEBEIAN
Poor soul, his eyes are red as fire with weeping.
THIRD PLEBEIAN
There's not a nobler man in Rome than Antony.
FOURTH PLEBEIAN
Now mark him. He begins again to speak.
ANTONY
But yesterday the word of Caesar might   130
Have stood against the world. Now lies he there,
And none so poor to do him reverence.
O masters, if I were disposed to stir
Your hearts and minds to mutiny and rage,
I should do Brutus wrong and Cassius wrong,   135
Who, you all know, are honorable men.
I will not do them wrong. I rather choose
To wrong the dead, to wrong myself and you,
Than I will wrong such honorable men.
But here's a parchment with the seal of Caesar.   140
I found it in his closet. 'Tis his will.
Let but the commons hear this testament,
Which, pardon me, I do not mean to read,
And they would go and kiss dead Caesar's wounds
And dip their napkins in his sacred blood—   145
Yea, beg a hair of him for memory
And, dying, mention it within their wills,
Bequeathing it as a rich legacy
Unto their issue.
FOURTH PLEBEIAN
We'll hear the will. Read it, Mark Antony.   150
PLEBEIANS
The will, the will! We will hear Caesar's will.
ANTONY
Have patience, gentle friends. I must not read it.

153. **meet:** appropriate

162. **o'ershot myself:** gone too far

177. **from:** away **from,** at a distance **from; hearse:** the bier on which the body was placed; or, the corpse itself

179. **far:** i.e., farther

It is not meet you know how Caesar loved you.
You are not wood, you are not stones, but men.
And, being men, hearing the will of Caesar,   155
It will inflame you; it will make you mad.
'Tis good you know not that you are his heirs,
For if you should, O, what would come of it?
FOURTH PLEBEIAN
  Read the will! We'll hear it, Antony.
⌜PLEBEIANS⌝
  You shall read us the will, Caesar's will.   160
ANTONY
  Will you be patient? Will you stay awhile?
  I have o'ershot myself to tell you of it.
  I fear I wrong the honorable men
  Whose daggers have stabbed Caesar. I do fear it.
FOURTH PLEBEIAN   They were traitors. Honorable men?   165
PLEBEIANS   The will! The testament!
SECOND PLEBEIAN   They were villains, murderers. The
  will! Read the will.
ANTONY
  You will compel me, then, to read the will?
  Then make a ring about the corpse of Caesar,   170
  And let me show you him that made the will.
  Shall I descend? And will you give me leave?
PLEBEIANS   Come down.
SECOND PLEBEIAN   Descend.
THIRD PLEBEIAN   You shall have leave.   175
                                    ⌜*Antony descends.*⌝
FOURTH PLEBEIAN   A ring; stand round.
FIRST PLEBEIAN
  Stand from the hearse. Stand from the body.
SECOND PLEBEIAN
  Room for Antony, most noble Antony.
ANTONY
  Nay, press not so upon me. Stand far off.

185. **Nervii:** a tribe conquered by Caesar in 57 B.C.E.

187. **rent:** rip, hole; **envious:** spiteful

191. **be resolved:** i.e., find out (literally, be freed from doubt or uncertainty)

193. **Caesar's angel:** i.e., as dear to Caesar as if he had been **Caesar's** "daemon" or guardian spirit

206. **dint:** force, stroke

207. **what:** an exclamation introducing a question

208. **vesture:** garment

209. **marred:** destroyed or mangled; **with:** by

PLEBEIANS   Stand back! Room! Bear back!   180
ANTONY
  If you have tears, prepare to shed them now.
  You all do know this mantle. I remember
  The first time ever Caesar put it on.
  'Twas on a summer's evening in his tent,
  That day he overcame the Nervii.   185
  Look, in this place ran Cassius' dagger through.
  See what a rent the envious Casca made.
  Through this the well-belovèd Brutus stabbed,
  And, as he plucked his cursèd steel away,
  Mark how the blood of Caesar followed it,   190
  As rushing out of doors to be resolved
  If Brutus so unkindly knocked or no;
  For Brutus, as you know, was Caesar's angel.
  Judge, O you gods, how dearly Caesar loved him!
  This was the most unkindest cut of all.   195
  For when the noble Caesar saw him stab,
  Ingratitude, more strong than traitors' arms,
  Quite vanquished him. Then burst his mighty heart,
  And, in his mantle muffling up his face,
  Even at the base of Pompey's statue   200
  (Which all the while ran blood) great Caesar fell.
  O, what a fall was there, my countrymen!
  Then I and you and all of us fell down,
  Whilst bloody treason flourished over us.
  O, now you weep, and I perceive you feel   205
  The dint of pity. These are gracious drops.
  Kind souls, what, weep you when you but behold
  Our Caesar's vesture wounded? Look you here,
                       ⌜*Antony lifts Caesar's cloak.*⌝
  Here is himself, marred as you see with traitors.
FIRST PLEBEIAN   O piteous spectacle!   210
SECOND PLEBEIAN   O noble Caesar!
THIRD PLEBEIAN   O woeful day!

223. **mutiny:** discord, contention
225. **griefs:** grievances
230. **blunt:** (1) dull, stupid; (2) plain-spoken
232. **public leave to speak:** permission **to speak**
publicly
233. **wit:** intellectual cleverness
240. **there were:** that would be
241. **ruffle up:** enrage
243. **mutiny:** revolt

FOURTH PLEBEIAN   O traitors, villains!
FIRST PLEBEIAN   O most bloody sight!
SECOND PLEBEIAN   We will be revenged.   215
⌈PLEBEIANS⌉   Revenge! About! Seek! Burn! Fire! Kill!
   Slay! Let not a traitor live!
ANTONY   Stay, countrymen.
FIRST PLEBEIAN   Peace there! Hear the noble Antony.
SECOND PLEBEIAN   We'll hear him, we'll follow him,   220
   we'll die with him.
ANTONY
   Good friends, sweet friends, let me not stir you up
   To such a sudden flood of mutiny.
   They that have done this deed are honorable.
   What private griefs they have, alas, I know not,   225
   That made them do it. They are wise and honorable
   And will no doubt with reasons answer you.
   I come not, friends, to steal away your hearts.
   I am no orator, as Brutus is,
   But, as you know me all, a plain blunt man   230
   That love my friend, and that they know full well
   That gave me public leave to speak of him.
   For I have neither ⌈wit,⌉ nor words, nor worth,
   Action, nor utterance, nor the power of speech
   To stir men's blood. I only speak right on.   235
   I tell you that which you yourselves do know,
   Show you sweet Caesar's wounds, poor poor dumb
      mouths,
   And bid them speak for me. But were I Brutus,
   And Brutus Antony, there were an Antony   240
   Would ruffle up your spirits and put a tongue
   In every wound of Caesar that should move
   The stones of Rome to rise and mutiny.
PLEBEIANS
   We'll mutiny.
FIRST PLEBEIAN   We'll burn the house of Brutus.   245

256. **several:** individual; **drachmas:** silver coins
261. **walks:** avenues for walking, promenades
262. **orchards:** gardens (See picture, page 50.)
264. **common:** public; **pleasures:** i.e., pleasure grounds, parks
265. **abroad:** out of doors
269. **brands:** firebrands, pieces of burning wood

THIRD PLEBEIAN
Away then. Come, seek the conspirators.
ANTONY
Yet hear me, countrymen; yet hear me speak.
PLEBEIANS
Peace, ho! Hear Antony, most noble Antony!
ANTONY
Why, friends, you go to do you know not what.
Wherein hath Caesar thus deserved your loves?   250
Alas, you know not. I must tell you then.
You have forgot the will I told you of.
PLEBEIANS
Most true. The will! Let's stay and hear the will.
ANTONY
Here is the will, and under Caesar's seal:
To every Roman citizen he gives,   255
To every several man, seventy-five drachmas.
SECOND PLEBEIAN
Most noble Caesar! We'll revenge his death.
THIRD PLEBEIAN   O royal Caesar!
ANTONY   Hear me with patience.
PLEBEIANS   Peace, ho!   260
ANTONY
Moreover, he hath left you all his walks,
His private arbors, and new-planted orchards,
On this side Tiber. He hath left them you,
And to your heirs forever—common pleasures
To walk abroad and recreate yourselves.   265
Here was a Caesar! When comes such another?
FIRST PLEBEIAN
Never, never!—Come, away, away!
We'll burn his body in the holy place
And with the brands fire the traitors' houses.
Take up the body.   270
SECOND PLEBEIAN   Go fetch fire.
THIRD PLEBEIAN   Pluck down benches.

273. **forms:** i.e., **benches; windows:** i.e., shutters

275. **Mischief:** (1) misfortune, trouble; (2) evil-doing, wickedness

281. **will I straight: I will** go immediately

282. **upon a wish:** i.e., opportunely, just at the right moment; **Fortune:** the goddess Fortuna, known for the whimsical way she dispenses good and bad luck (See picture, page 136.)

285. **Are rid:** have ridden

286. **Belike:** probably

286–87. **some notice . . . them:** i.e., news of **how I had** stirred the people's emotions

3.3 Cinna the poet is attacked and killed by the Roman mob because his name is the same as that of one of the conspirators.

---

1. **tonight:** last night

2. **unluckily charge my fantasy:** i.e., burden my imagination with bad omens

3. **forth of doors:** i.e., out **of doors**

FOURTH PLEBEIAN Pluck down forms, windows, anything.

Plebeians exit ⌈with Caesar's body.⌉

ANTONY
Now let it work. Mischief, thou art afoot;   275
Take thou what course thou wilt.

Enter Servant.

How now, fellow?

SERVANT
Sir, Octavius is already come to Rome.

ANTONY Where is he?

SERVANT
He and Lepidus are at Caesar's house.   280

ANTONY
And thither will I straight to visit him.
He comes upon a wish. Fortune is merry
And in this mood will give us anything.

SERVANT
I heard him say Brutus and Cassius
Are rid like madmen through the gates of Rome.   285

ANTONY
Belike they had some notice of the people
How I had moved them. Bring me to Octavius.

They exit.

⌈Scene 3⌉

Enter Cinna the poet and after him the Plebeians.

CINNA
I dreamt tonight that I did feast with Caesar,
And things unluckily charge my fantasy.
I have no will to wander forth of doors,
Yet something leads me forth.

FIRST PLEBEIAN What is your name?   5

13. **you were best:** i.e., if you know what's good for you

19. **bear me a bang:** get a blow from me

35–36. **turn him going:** send him away (i.e., kill him)

38. **Brutus':** Brutus's house

The Goddess Fortuna. (3.2.282)
From Gregor Reisch, *Margarita philosophica* . . . (1503).

SECOND PLEBEIAN Whither are you going?

THIRD PLEBEIAN Where do you dwell?

FOURTH PLEBEIAN Are you a married man or a bachelor?

SECOND PLEBEIAN Answer every man directly.   10

FIRST PLEBEIAN Ay, and briefly.

FOURTH PLEBEIAN Ay, and wisely.

THIRD PLEBEIAN Ay, and truly, you were best.

CINNA What is my name? Whither am I going? Where do I dwell? Am I a married man or a bachelor?   15
Then to answer every man directly and briefly, wisely and truly: wisely I say, I am a bachelor.

SECOND PLEBEIAN That's as much as to say they are fools that marry. You'll bear me a bang for that, I fear. Proceed directly.   20

CINNA Directly, I am going to Caesar's funeral.

FIRST PLEBEIAN As a friend or an enemy?

CINNA As a friend.

SECOND PLEBEIAN That matter is answered directly.

FOURTH PLEBEIAN For your dwelling—briefly.   25

CINNA Briefly, I dwell by the Capitol.

THIRD PLEBEIAN Your name, sir, truly.

CINNA Truly, my name is Cinna.

FIRST PLEBEIAN Tear him to pieces! He's a conspirator.

CINNA I am Cinna the poet, I am Cinna the poet!   30

FOURTH PLEBEIAN Tear him for his bad verses, tear him for his bad verses!

CINNA I am not Cinna the conspirator.

FOURTH PLEBEIAN It is no matter. His name's Cinna. Pluck but his name out of his heart, and turn him   35
going.

THIRD PLEBEIAN Tear him, tear him! Come, brands, ho, firebrands! To Brutus', to Cassius', burn all! Some to Decius' house, and some to Casca's, some to Ligarius'. Away, go!   40

All the Plebeians exit, ⌐carrying off Cinna.⌐

The Tragedy of

JULIUS CAESAR

ACT 4

4.1 Antony, Lepidus, and Octavius meet to condemn to death those who may oppose them. Sending Lepidus for Caesar's will, Antony expresses contempt for Lepidus and plans with Octavius to raise an army to fight the troops of Brutus and Cassius.

---

2. **pricked:** marked for death with a pinprick or dot

3. **Lepidus:** Closely allied with Julius Caesar, **Lepidus** supported Antony's bid for power and joined Antony and Octavius in forming the Second Triumvirate, which marked the end of the Roman Republic.

8. **damn:** condemn

11. **cut . . . legacies:** reduce some of the will's bequests

12. **What:** an exclamation introducing a question

13. **Or . . . or:** either . . . **or**

14. **slight, unmeritable:** of little value, undeserving

15. **Meet:** suitable; **fit:** fitting

16. **The threefold world divided:** i.e., in our dividing of the Roman **world** among the three of us; **stand:** i.e., be

ACT 4

⌜Scene 1⌝

Enter Antony, Octavius, and Lepidus.

ANTONY
These many, then, shall die; their names are
  pricked.
OCTAVIUS
Your brother too must die. Consent you, Lepidus?
LEPIDUS
I do consent.
OCTAVIUS   Prick him down, Antony.   5
LEPIDUS
Upon condition Publius shall not live,
Who is your sister's son, Mark Antony.
ANTONY
He shall not live; look, with a spot I damn him.
But, Lepidus, go you to Caesar's house;
Fetch the will hither, and we shall determine   10
How to cut off some charge in legacies.
LEPIDUS What, shall I find you here?
OCTAVIUS Or here, or at the Capitol.   *Lepidus exits.*
ANTONY
This is a slight, unmeritable man,
Meet to be sent on errands. Is it fit,   15
The threefold world divided, he should stand
One of the three to share it?

141

19. **voice:** vote, opinion

20. **black sentence and proscription:** i.e., **sentence** of death

23. **sland'rous loads:** burdens that would discredit or shame us

24. **bear:** own, possess, display (as an ornament); **bears:** carries as a burden (For picture of an **ass** bearing a burden, see page 158.)

27. **where we will:** i.e., **where we** want it to go

30. **commons:** public pasture

34. **appoint:** grant; **store:** a supply

36. **wind:** turn

38. **in some taste:** i.e., to **some** degree

40–43. **one . . . fashion:** i.e., **one** who chooses as fashionable only things already out of **fashion   out of use:** no longer in **use   staled:** cheapened

44. **property:** means to an end, tool

45. **Listen:** i.e., **listen** to; **great:** important

46. **powers:** troops; **straight:** immediately; **make head:** raise an army; or, press forward

47. **let . . . combined: let our** allies **be** joined together

48. **made:** gathered

49. **sit in council:** i.e., discuss, deliberate about

51. **surest answerèd:** most safely encountered

OCTAVIUS   So you thought him
  And took his voice who should be pricked to die
  In our black sentence and proscription.   20
ANTONY
  Octavius, I have seen more days than you,
  And, though we lay these honors on this man
  To ease ourselves of diverse sland'rous loads,
  He shall but bear them as the ass bears gold,
  To groan and sweat under the business,   25
  Either led or driven, as we point the way;
  And having brought our treasure where we will,
  Then take we down his load and turn him off
  (Like to the empty ass) to shake his ears
  And graze in commons.   30
OCTAVIUS   You may do your will,
  But he's a tried and valiant soldier.
ANTONY
  So is my horse, Octavius, and for that
  I do appoint him store of provender.
  It is a creature that I teach to fight,   35
  To wind, to stop, to run directly on,
  His corporal motion governed by my spirit;
  And, in some taste, is Lepidus but so.
  He must be taught and trained and bid go forth—
  A barren-spirited fellow, one that feeds   40
  On objects, arts, and imitations
  Which, out of use and staled by other men,
  Begin his fashion. Do not talk of him
  But as a property. And now, Octavius,
  Listen great things. Brutus and Cassius   45
  Are levying powers. We must straight make head.
  Therefore let our alliance be combined,
  Our best friends made, our means stretched;
  And let us presently go sit in council
  How covert matters may be best disclosed   50
  And open perils surest answerèd.

52–53. at the stake / And bayed about: i.e., like the bear in a bearbaiting, tied to **the stake** and surrounded by attacking dogs (See picture, page 152.)

55. mischiefs: evil deeds

4.2 Brutus and Cassius each feel wronged by the other. They prepare to withdraw from the view of their armies to resolve their dispute privately in Brutus's tent.

---

0 SD. Enter Brutus, Lucilius. . . . Titinius and Pindarus meet them: Despite the Folio entrance directions, the dialogue suggests that Lucilius enters with Titinius and Pindarus.

1. Stand: halt

6. He . . . well: i.e., he has sent a good ambassador

7. In his own change: perhaps, because he has changed; **ill:** bad

8. worthy: justifiable

10. be satisfied: receive a satisfactory explanation

16. resolved: fully informed

18. familiar instances: signs of friendship

19. conference: conversation

OCTAVIUS
Let us do so, for we are at the stake
And bayed about with many enemies,
And some that smile have in their hearts, I fear,
Millions of mischiefs.   55
They exit.

⌜Scene 2⌝

Drum. Enter Brutus, Lucilius, ⌜Lucius,⌝ and the Army.
Titinius and Pindarus meet them.

BRUTUS Stand ho!
LUCILIUS Give the word, ho, and stand!
BRUTUS
What now, Lucilius, is Cassius near?
LUCILIUS
He is at hand, and Pindarus is come
To do you salutation from his master.   5
BRUTUS
He greets me well.—Your master, Pindarus,
In his own change or by ill officers,
Hath given me some worthy cause to wish
Things done undone, but if he be at hand
I shall be satisfied.   10
PINDARUS   I do not doubt
But that my noble master will appear
Such as he is, full of regard and honor.
BRUTUS
He is not doubted. ⌜*Brutus and Lucilius walk aside.*⌝
A word, Lucilius,   15
How he received you. Let me be resolved.
LUCILIUS
With courtesy and with respect enough,
But not with such familiar instances
Nor with such free and friendly conference
As he hath used of old.   20

24. **enforcèd:** forced, unnatural

26. **hot at hand:** fiery at the start

29. **fall their crests:** let **fall their** manes, or their necks (i.e., drop their pretense of fieriness); **jades:** broken-down horses (See picture, below.) The word *jade* also meant "worthless or fickle woman," and may carry that sense here.

30. **Sink in the trial:** fail when put to the test

31. **Sardis:** an ancient city in present-day Turkey

32. **the horse in general:** all of the cavalry

35. **gently:** with noble bearing; or, slowly

44. **this sober form of yours:** your solemn, dignified manner

47. **griefs:** grievances

Horse letting fall its crest. (4.2.29)
From Cesare Fiaschi, *Trattato dell'imbrigliare . . . caualli . . .* (1614).

BRUTUS   Thou hast described
A hot friend cooling. Ever note, Lucilius,
When love begins to sicken and decay
It useth an enforcèd ceremony.
There are no tricks in plain and simple faith;   25
But hollow men, like horses hot at hand,
Make gallant show and promise of their mettle,
                    Low march within.
But when they should endure the bloody spur,
They fall their crests and, like deceitful jades,
Sink in the trial. Comes his army on?   30
LUCILIUS
They mean this night in Sardis to be quartered.
The greater part, the horse in general,
Are come with Cassius.

                Enter Cassius and his powers.

BRUTUS   Hark, he is arrived.
March gently on to meet him.   35
CASSIUS Stand ho!
BRUTUS Stand ho! Speak the word along.
⌜FIRST SOLDIER⌝ Stand!
⌜SECOND SOLDIER⌝ Stand!
⌜THIRD SOLDIER⌝ Stand!   40
CASSIUS
Most noble brother, you have done me wrong.
BRUTUS
Judge me, you gods! Wrong I mine enemies?
And if not so, how should I wrong a brother?
CASSIUS
Brutus, this sober form of yours hides wrongs,
And when you do them—   45
BRUTUS   Cassius, be content.
Speak your griefs softly. I do know you well.
Before the eyes of both our armies here
(Which should perceive nothing but love from us),

4.3 Brutus and Cassius exchange accusations in Brutus's tent. They grow angry with each other but are quickly reconciled, and Brutus tells Cassius of Portia's death. With Titinius and Messala they plot their military strategy. Brutus overrides Cassius's objections and insists that they march to Philippi to challenge Mark Antony and Octavius. As Brutus reads in his tent after the meeting, he is visited by the Ghost of Caesar, who threatens to visit Brutus again at Philippi.

---

1. The action of the play is continuous from 4.2 to 4.3, and Brutus and Cassius remain onstage. Therefore there may seem to be no cause for scene division here. However, there is emphasis on a marked change of location from the field (4.2) to the privacy of Brutus's tent (4.3). Since a change of location is usually marked by scene division, most editors begin a new scene at this point.

2. **noted:** publicly disgraced

3. **Sardians:** See note to **Sardis** at 4.2.31.

4. **letters:** i.e., letter (Latin *litterae*); **praying . . . side:** i.e., entreating you on his behalf

8. **nice:** petty; **bear his comment:** receive notice **his:** i.e., its

10. **condemned to have:** accused of having; **an itching palm:** an old phrase that describes a person greedy for money (See picture, page 154.)

11. **mart:** traffic in; **offices:** services

16. **honors this corruption:** i.e., gives a kind of credit to such corrupt practices

17. **chastisement . . . head:** i.e., corrupt officers go unpunished

Let us not wrangle. Bid them move away.　　　50
Then in my tent, Cassius, enlarge your griefs,
And I will give you audience.
CASSIUS　　　　　　　　　　　Pindarus,
Bid our commanders lead their charges off
A little from this ground.　　　　　　　55
BRUTUS
⌐Lucius,⌐ do you the like, and let no man
Come to our tent till we have done our conference.
Let ⌐Lucilius⌐ and Titinius guard our door.
　　　　　　　All but Brutus and Cassius exit.

　　　　　　　⌐Scene 3⌐
CASSIUS
That you have wronged me doth appear in this:
You have condemned and noted Lucius Pella
For taking bribes here of the Sardians,
Wherein my letters, praying on his side
Because I knew the man, was slighted off.　　　5
BRUTUS
You wronged yourself to write in such a case.
CASSIUS
In such a time as this it is not meet
That every nice offense should bear his comment.
BRUTUS
Let me tell you, Cassius, you yourself
Are much condemned to have an itching palm,　　　10
To sell and mart your offices for gold
To undeservers.
CASSIUS　　　　　I an itching palm?
You know that you are Brutus that speaks this,
Or, by the gods, this speech were else your last.　　　15
BRUTUS
The name of Cassius honors this corruption,
And chastisement doth therefore hide his head.

24. **But . . . robbers:** only for tolerating dishonesty (a reason for the assassination of Caesar not mentioned before)

27. **trash:** i.e., money

28. **bay:** bark at (See picture, below.)

30. **bait:** attack (as dogs do the bear in bearbaiting) See picture, page 152.

34. **make conditions:** i.e., manage affairs (literally, make terms)

38. **Urge:** provoke

43. **choler:** anger

48. **budge:** wince, flinch

Dog baying the moon. (4.3.28)
From Geoffrey Whitney, *A choice of emblemes . . .* (1586).

CASSIUS Chastisement?

BRUTUS

Remember March; the ides of March remember.
Did not great Julius bleed for justice' sake?   20
What villain touched his body that did stab
And not for justice? What, shall one of us
That struck the foremost man of all this world
But for supporting robbers, shall we now
Contaminate our fingers with base bribes   25
And sell the mighty space of our large honors
For so much trash as may be graspèd thus?
I had rather be a dog and bay the moon
Than such a Roman.

CASSIUS   Brutus, bait not me.   30
I'll not endure it. You forget yourself
To hedge me in. I am a soldier, I,
Older in practice, abler than yourself
To make conditions.

BRUTUS   Go to! You are not, Cassius.   35

CASSIUS I am.

BRUTUS I say you are not.

CASSIUS

Urge me no more. I shall forget myself.
Have mind upon your health. Tempt me no farther.

BRUTUS Away, slight man!   40

CASSIUS

Is 't possible?

BRUTUS   Hear me, for I will speak.
Must I give way and room to your rash choler?
Shall I be frighted when a madman stares?

CASSIUS

O you gods, you gods, must I endure all this?   45

BRUTUS

All this? Ay, more. Fret till your proud heart break.
Go show your slaves how choleric you are
And make your bondmen tremble. Must I budge?

49. **observe:** show respect to

51. **digest . . . spleen:** swallow down the poison of your angry temper (i.e., keep your anger to yourself)

57. **vaunting:** boasting

59. **of noble men:** perhaps, that **men** can be **noble;** or, perhaps, from **noble men** (like you)

64. **moved:** angered

66. **tempted:** provoked

73, 74. **that:** i.e., **that** which

76. **honesty:** my own honor and reputation; integrity

A bear "at the stake and bayed about." (4.1.52–53; 4.3.30)
From William Lily, *Antibossicon . . .* (1521).

Must I observe you? Must I stand and crouch
Under your testy humor? By the gods,   50
You shall digest the venom of your spleen
Though it do split you. For, from this day forth,
I'll use you for my mirth, yea, for my laughter,
When you are waspish.
CASSIUS   Is it come to this?   55
BRUTUS
You say you are a better soldier.
Let it appear so, make your vaunting true,
And it shall please me well. For mine own part,
I shall be glad to learn of noble men.
CASSIUS
You wrong me every way, you wrong me, Brutus.   60
I said an elder soldier, not a better.
Did I say "better"?
BRUTUS   If you did, I care not.
CASSIUS
When Caesar lived he durst not thus have moved
  me.   65
BRUTUS
Peace, peace! You durst not so have tempted him.
CASSIUS   I durst not?
BRUTUS   No.
CASSIUS
What? Durst not tempt him?
BRUTUS   For your life you durst   70
  not.
CASSIUS
Do not presume too much upon my love.
I may do that I shall be sorry for.
BRUTUS
You have done that you should be sorry for.
There is no terror, Cassius, in your threats,   75
For I am armed so strong in honesty
That they pass by me as the idle wind,

83. **trash:** i.e., money

84. **indirection:** deceitful means

87. **Should:** would

89. **To lock . . . counters;** i.e., as **to lock such** petty tokens (**Counters** were worthless tokens; the word came to be used to refer with contempt to money.)

94–95. **He . . . back:** i.e., the messenger misrepresented **my answer**

103. **Olympus:** Mount **Olympus**, the highest point in Greece (See note to 3.1.81.)

107. **braved:** threatened

"An itching palm." (4.3.10)
From John Bulwer, *Chirologia* . . . (1644).

Which I respect not. I did send to you
For certain sums of gold, which you denied me,
For I can raise no money by vile means.   80
By heaven, I had rather coin my heart
And drop my blood for drachmas than to wring
From the hard hands of peasants their vile trash
By any indirection. I did send
To you for gold to pay my legions,   85
Which you denied me. Was that done like Cassius?
Should I have answered Caius Cassius so?
When Marcus Brutus grows so covetous
To lock such rascal counters from his friends,
Be ready, gods, with all your thunderbolts;   90
Dash him to pieces!
CASSIUS   I denied you not.
BRUTUS You did.
CASSIUS
I did not. He was but a fool that brought
My answer back. Brutus hath rived my heart.   95
A friend should bear his friend's infirmities,
But Brutus makes mine greater than they are.
BRUTUS
I do not, till you practice them on me.
CASSIUS
You love me not.
BRUTUS   I do not like your faults.   100
CASSIUS
A friendly eye could never see such faults.
BRUTUS
A flatterer's would not, though they do appear
As huge as high Olympus.
CASSIUS
Come, Antony, and young Octavius, come!
Revenge yourselves alone on Cassius,   105
For Cassius is aweary of the world—
Hated by one he loves, braved by his brother,

108. **Checked:** rebuked; **bondman:** slave

109. **conned by rote:** memorized

113. **Dearer . . . mine:** more precious than the gold and silver mines in the realm of Pluto, god of the underworld, who here, as often, has been identified with Plutus, the god of wealth

115. **I . . . gold:** i.e., **I** who, according to you, **denied** you **gold**

122. **scope:** free play

123. **dishonor . . . humor:** i.e., (1) I will pass off your insults to me as the result of your bad mood; or (2) I will regard your dishonorable actions as mere caprice

126. **much enforcèd:** struck hard (in reference to the flint); strongly provoked (in reference to his lamblike self)

127. **straight:** immediately

130. **blood ill-tempered:** a disposition that is badly "tempered," unbalanced (with a play on **ill-tempered** as "bad humored")

137. **that rash humor:** i.e., anger; **my mother gave me:** Here, as often in Shakespeare, a man explains his inconstant or weak characteristics as the result of his descent from a woman as well as from a man. Cassius describes his rashness as an effeminate trait in himself inherited from his **mother.**

Checked like a bondman, all his faults observed,
Set in a notebook, learned and conned by rote
To cast into my teeth. O, I could weep   110
My spirit from mine eyes! There is my dagger,
                    ⌜*Offering his dagger to Brutus.*⌝
And here my naked breast; within, a heart
Dearer than Pluto's mine, richer than gold.
If that thou be'st a Roman, take it forth.
I that denied thee gold will give my heart.   115
Strike as thou didst at Caesar, for I know
When thou didst hate him worst, thou lovedst him
    better
Than ever thou lovedst Cassius.
BRUTUS   Sheathe your   120
    dagger.
Be angry when you will, it shall have scope.
Do what you will, dishonor shall be humor.
O Cassius, you are yokèd with a lamb
That carries anger as the flint bears fire,   125
Who, much enforcèd, shows a hasty spark
And straight is cold again.
CASSIUS   Hath Cassius lived
To be but mirth and laughter to his Brutus
When grief and blood ill-tempered vexeth him?   130
BRUTUS
When I spoke that, I was ill-tempered too.
CASSIUS
Do you confess so much? Give me your hand.
BRUTUS
And my heart too.   ⌜*They clasp hands.*⌝
CASSIUS   O Brutus!
BRUTUS   What's the matter?   135
CASSIUS
Have not you love enough to bear with me
When that rash humor which my mother gave me
Makes me forgetful?

144. **meet:** fitting

152. **cynic:** scoffer (The word also designates a kind of philosopher, a **Cynic,** who advocates extreme asceticism.)

156. **jigging:** rhyming

157. **Companion:** fellow (here, a term of contempt)

An ass bearing a burden. (4.1.24)
From Geoffrey Whitney, *A choice of emblemes . . .* (1586).

BRUTUS   Yes, Cassius, and from
  henceforth   140
When you are over-earnest with your Brutus,
He'll think your mother chides, and leave you so.

Enter a Poet ⌜followed by Lucilius, Titinius, and Lucius.⌝

POET
Let me go in to see the Generals.
There is some grudge between 'em; 'tis not meet
They be alone.   145
LUCILIUS   You shall not come to them.
POET Nothing but death shall stay me.
CASSIUS How now, what's the matter?
POET
For shame, you generals, what do you mean?
Love and be friends as two such men should be,   150
For I have seen more years, I'm sure, than ye.
CASSIUS
Ha, ha, how vilely doth this cynic rhyme!
BRUTUS
Get you hence, sirrah! Saucy fellow, hence!
CASSIUS
Bear with him, Brutus. 'Tis his fashion.
BRUTUS
I'll know his humor when he knows his time.   155
What should the wars do with these jigging fools?—
Companion, hence!
CASSIUS   Away, away, be gone! *Poet exits.*
BRUTUS
Lucilius and Titinius, bid the commanders
Prepare to lodge their companies tonight.   160
CASSIUS
And come yourselves, and bring Messala with you
Immediately to us.   ⌜*Lucilius and Titinius exit.*⌝
BRUTUS Lucius, a bowl of wine.   ⌜*Lucius exits.*⌝

166. **your philosophy:** i.e., Stoicism, which taught that one should view the ups and downs of life with detachment

167. **give place to: give** in **to; accidental evils:** misfortunes brought about by chance

173. **Upon:** of

174. **Impatient of:** unable to endure

176–77. **her death:** i.e., the news of **her death**

179. **fire:** i.e., burning coals

185. **pledge:** toast; promise

CASSIUS
I did not think you could have been so angry.
BRUTUS
O Cassius, I am sick of many griefs.   165
CASSIUS
Of your philosophy you make no use
If you give place to accidental evils.
BRUTUS
No man bears sorrow better. Portia is dead.
CASSIUS Ha? Portia?
BRUTUS She is dead.   170
CASSIUS
How 'scaped I killing when I crossed you so?
O insupportable and touching loss!
Upon what sickness?
BRUTUS   Impatient of my absence,
And grief that young Octavius with Mark Antony   175
Have made themselves so strong—for with her
    death
That tidings came—with this she fell distract
And, her attendants absent, swallowed fire.
CASSIUS And died so?   180
BRUTUS Even so.
CASSIUS O you immortal gods!

          Enter ⌐Lucius⌐ with wine and tapers.

BRUTUS
Speak no more of her.—Give me a bowl of wine.—
In this I bury all unkindness, Cassius.   ⌐He⌐ drinks.
CASSIUS
My heart is thirsty for that noble pledge.—   185
Fill, Lucius, till the wine o'erswell the cup;
I cannot drink too much of Brutus' love. ⌐He drinks.⌐
                              ⌐Lucius exits.⌐

          Enter Titinius and Messala.

190. **call in question:** discuss

196. **Philippi:** accent on second syllable (The meter here and throughout demands this pronunciation.) See map, page 172.

208–23. **Had you your . . . bear it so:** This second revelation of Portia's death raises significant questions, given Brutus's earlier disclosure of her death to Cassius in lines 168–83. It is possible that lines 208–23 were supposed to have been canceled and that lines 168–83 were designed to replace the public revelation with a private one. With lines 208–23 deleted, line 224 ("Well, to our work alive") would refer to Cicero's, rather than Portia's, death.

Cicero. (1.2.0 SD, 195, 289; 1.3; 2.1.152–66; 4.3.204–6)
From [Guillaume Rouillé,] . . . *Promptuarii iconum* . . . (1553).

BRUTUS
Come in, Titinius. Welcome, good Messala.
Now sit we close about this taper here,
And call in question our necessities. ⌜*They sit.*⌝ 190
CASSIUS
Portia, art thou gone?
BRUTUS   No more, I pray you.—
Messala, I have here receivèd letters
That young Octavius and Mark Antony
Come down upon us with a mighty power, 195
Bending their expedition toward Philippi.
MESSALA
Myself have letters of the selfsame tenor.
BRUTUS   With what addition?
MESSALA
That by proscription and bills of outlawry,
Octavius, Antony, and Lepidus 200
Have put to death an hundred senators.
BRUTUS
Therein our letters do not well agree.
Mine speak of seventy senators that died
By their proscriptions, Cicero being one.
CASSIUS
Cicero one? 205
MESSALA   Cicero is dead,
And by that order of proscription.
Had you your letters from your wife, my lord?
BRUTUS   No, Messala.
MESSALA
Nor nothing in your letters writ of her? 210
BRUTUS
Nothing, Messala.
MESSALA   That methinks is strange.
BRUTUS
Why ask you? Hear you aught of her in yours?
MESSALA   No, my lord.

219. **once:** at some time, one day
222. **in art:** in theory
224. **to our work alive:** i.e., let us get about the **work** that faces us who are **alive**
225. **presently:** immediately
231. **offense:** harm
233. **of force:** necessarily
235. **Do . . . affection:** are loyal to us only because we force them to be
239. **new-added:** reinforced
240. **him:** i.e., the enemy force

BRUTUS
　Now, as you are a Roman, tell me true.   215
MESSALA
　Then like a Roman bear the truth I tell,
　For certain she is dead, and by strange manner.
BRUTUS
　Why, farewell, Portia. We must die, Messala.
　With meditating that she must die once,
　I have the patience to endure it now.   220
MESSALA
　Even so great men great losses should endure.
CASSIUS
　I have as much of this in art as you,
　But yet my nature could not bear it so.
BRUTUS
　Well, to our work alive. What do you think
　Of marching to Philippi presently?   225
CASSIUS　I do not think it good.
BRUTUS　Your reason?
CASSIUS　This it is:
　'Tis better that the enemy seek us;
　So shall he waste his means, weary his soldiers,   230
　Doing himself offense, whilst we, lying still,
　Are full of rest, defense, and nimbleness.
BRUTUS
　Good reasons must of force give place to better.
　The people 'twixt Philippi and this ground
　Do stand but in a forced affection,   235
　For they have grudged us contribution.
　The enemy, marching along by them,
　By them shall make a fuller number up,
　Come on refreshed, new-added, and encouraged,
　From which advantage shall we cut him off   240
　If at Philippi we do face him there,
　These people at our back.
CASSIUS　　　　　　　　Hear me, good brother—

244. **Under your pardon:** i.e., begging **your pardon,** I will continue

245. **tried the utmost of our friends:** demanded from **our friends** all they can provide

250. **at the flood:** as it is flowing in

251. **Omitted:** ignored; not taken

252. **bound in:** confined to

255. **ventures:** merchandise ventured in trade

256. **with your will:** as you wish

260. **Which . . . rest:** i.e., **we will** supply nature's need of sleep by resting briefly **niggard:** supply sparingly

263. **hence:** i.e., go **hence**

BRUTUS
  Under your pardon. You must note besides
  That we have tried the utmost of our friends,   245
  Our legions are brim full, our cause is ripe.
  The enemy increaseth every day;
  We, at the height, are ready to decline.
  There is a tide in the affairs of men
  Which, taken at the flood, leads on to fortune;   250
  Omitted, all the voyage of their life
  Is bound in shallows and in miseries.
  On such a full sea are we now afloat,
  And we must take the current when it serves
  Or lose our ventures.   255
CASSIUS   Then, with your will, go on;
  We'll along ourselves and meet them at Philippi.
BRUTUS
  The deep of night is crept upon our talk,
  And nature must obey necessity,
  Which we will niggard with a little rest.   260
  There is no more to say.
CASSIUS   No more. Good night.
                    ⌐*They stand.*¬
  Early tomorrow will we rise and hence.
BRUTUS
  Lucius.

Enter Lucius.

    My gown.   ⌐*Lucius exits.*¬ 265
        Farewell, good Messala.—
  Good night, Titinius.—Noble, noble Cassius,
  Good night and good repose.
CASSIUS   O my dear brother,
  This was an ill beginning of the night.   270
  Never come such division 'tween our souls!
  Let it not, Brutus.

Enter Lucius with the gown.

281. **o'erwatched:** tired from lack of sleep
289–90. **watch your pleasure:** i.e., keep watch and await your commands

Army camp at night. (4.2–4.3)
From Jacobus à Bruck, *Emblemata moralia & bellica* . . . (1615).

BRUTUS   Everything is well.
CASSIUS Good night, my lord.
BRUTUS Good night, good brother.   275
TITINIUS/MESSALA
  Good night, Lord Brutus.
BRUTUS   Farewell, everyone.
          ⌜*All but Brutus and Lucius*⌝ *exit.*
  Give me the gown. Where is thy instrument?
LUCIUS
  Here in the tent.
BRUTUS   What, thou speak'st drowsily?   280
  Poor knave, I blame thee not; thou art o'erwatched.
  Call Claudius and some other of my men;
  I'll have them sleep on cushions in my tent.
LUCIUS Varro and Claudius.

          Enter Varro and Claudius.

VARRO Calls my lord?   285
BRUTUS
  I pray you, sirs, lie in my tent and sleep.
  It may be I shall raise you by and by
  On business to my brother Cassius.
VARRO
  So please you, we will stand and watch your
    pleasure.   290
BRUTUS
  I will not have it so. Lie down, good sirs.
  It may be I shall otherwise bethink me.
                              ⌜*They lie down.*⌝
  Look, Lucius, here's the book I sought for so.
  I put it in the pocket of my gown.
LUCIUS
  I was sure your lordship did not give it me.   295
BRUTUS
  Bear with me, good boy, I am much forgetful.

298. **touch:** play on

304. **young bloods:** i.e., **young** bodies

310. **Layest . . . mace:** The image is of an officer (here, **slumber**) touching the shoulder of the person he is arresting with his heavy staff of office (**mace**).

311. **knave:** boy employed as a servant

323. **stare:** stand on end

Canst thou hold up thy heavy eyes awhile
And touch thy instrument a strain or two?

LUCIUS
Ay, my lord, an 't please you.

BRUTUS   It does, my boy.   300
I trouble thee too much, but thou art willing.

LUCIUS   It is my duty, sir.

BRUTUS
I should not urge thy duty past thy might.
I know young bloods look for a time of rest.

LUCIUS   I have slept, my lord, already.   305

BRUTUS
It was well done, and thou shalt sleep again.
I will not hold thee long. If I do live,
I will be good to thee.
              Music and a song. ⌜*Lucius then falls asleep.*⌝
This is a sleepy tune. O murd'rous ⌜slumber,⌝
Layest thou thy leaden mace upon my boy,   310
That plays thee music?—Gentle knave, good night.
I will not do thee so much wrong to wake thee.
If thou dost nod, thou break'st thy instrument.
I'll take it from thee and, good boy, good night.
                    ⌜*He moves the instrument.*⌝
Let me see, let me see; is not the leaf turned down   315
Where I left reading? Here it is, I think.
How ill this taper burns.

              Enter the Ghost of Caesar.

                    Ha, who comes here?—
I think it is the weakness of mine eyes
That shapes this monstrous apparition.   320
It comes upon me.—Art thou any thing?
Art thou some god, some angel, or some devil,
That mak'st my blood cold and my hair to stare?
Speak to me what thou art.

335. **false:** out of tune

343, 344. **Sirrah**, **Fellow:** These terms of address emphasize the inferior rank of **Claudius** and **Varro**.

A map of part of the Roman world.
Stephen Llano, based on John Speed, *A prospect of the most famous parts of the world . . .* (1631).

GHOST
   Thy evil spirit, Brutus.   325
BRUTUS   Why com'st thou?
GHOST
   To tell thee thou shalt see me at Philippi.
BRUTUS Well, then I shall see thee again?
GHOST Ay, at Philippi.
BRUTUS
   Why, I will see thee at Philippi, then.   ⌜*Ghost exits.*⌝ 330
   Now I have taken heart, thou vanishest.
   Ill spirit, I would hold more talk with thee.—
   Boy, Lucius!—Varro, Claudius, sirs, awake!
   Claudius!
LUCIUS   The strings, my lord, are false.   335
BRUTUS
   He thinks he still is at his instrument.
   Lucius, awake!
LUCIUS My lord?
BRUTUS
   Didst thou dream, Lucius, that thou so criedst out?
LUCIUS
   My lord, I do not know that I did cry.   340
BRUTUS
   Yes, that thou didst. Didst thou see anything?
LUCIUS Nothing, my lord.
BRUTUS
   Sleep again, Lucius.—Sirrah Claudius!
   ⌜*To Varro.*⌝ Fellow thou, awake!   ⌜*They rise up.*⌝
VARRO My lord?   345
CLAUDIUS My lord?
BRUTUS
   Why did you so cry out, sirs, in your sleep?
BOTH
   Did we, my lord?
BRUTUS   Ay. Saw you anything?
VARRO No, my lord, I saw nothing.   350

352. **commend me:** take my good wishes

353. **set . . . before:** advance his forces early this morning before me

CLAUDIUS Nor I, my lord.

BRUTUS

  Go and commend me to my brother Cassius.
  Bid him set on his powers betimes before,
  And we will follow.

BOTH   It shall be done, my lord.   355

                            They exit.

The Tragedy of

JULIUS CAESAR

ACT 5

5.1 The opposing armies confront each other at Philippi. Before the battle, Brutus and Cassius exchange insults with Antony and Octavius. Cassius is troubled by an omen of defeat, and he and Brutus say farewell in case they die as a result of the upcoming battle.

---

4. **battles:** battle forces, armies
5. **warn:** resist
7. **am in their bosoms:** i.e., know their secrets
8. **Wherefore:** why
8–9. **could . . . places:** i.e., would happily be someplace else
10. **fearful:** full of fear; or, fear-inspiring; **bravery:** ostentation, showiness; or, bravado; **face:** outward show
15. **bloody:** blood-red; **sign:** signal
17. **softly:** slowly

ACT 5

————————————————————————

⌜Scene 1⌝

Enter Octavius, Antony, and their army.

OCTAVIUS
Now, Antony, our hopes are answerèd.
You said the enemy would not come down
But keep the hills and upper regions.
It proves not so; their battles are at hand.
They mean to warn us at Philippi here,   5
Answering before we do demand of them.

ANTONY
Tut, I am in their bosoms, and I know
Wherefore they do it. They could be content
To visit other places, and come down
With fearful bravery, thinking by this face   10
To fasten in our thoughts that they have courage.
But 'tis not so.

Enter a Messenger.

MESSENGER   Prepare you, generals.
The enemy comes on in gallant show.
Their bloody sign of battle is hung out,   15
And something to be done immediately.

ANTONY
Octavius, lead your battle softly on
Upon the left hand of the even field.

179

20. **cross:** oppose; **exigent:** crucial occasion

21. **do so:** i.e., **do** as I said

25. **on their charge:** i.e., when they attack

35. **posture of your blows:** i.e., kinds **of blows** you will give

36. **for:** as for; **Hybla:** a place in ancient Sicily, famous for its honey (Cassius seems to refer to Antony's sweet words to the conspirators after the assassination.)

A kite. (5.1.92)
From Konrad Gesner, . . . *Historiae animalium* . . . (1585–1604).

OCTAVIUS
Upon the right hand, I; keep thou the left.
ANTONY
Why do you cross me in this exigent?   20
OCTAVIUS
I do not cross you, but I will do so.   *March.*

Drum. Enter Brutus, Cassius, and their army ⌐including
Lucilius, Titinius, and Messala.⌐

BRUTUS   They stand and would have parley.
CASSIUS
Stand fast, Titinius. We must out and talk.
OCTAVIUS
Mark Antony, shall we give sign of battle?
ANTONY
No, Caesar, we will answer on their charge.   25
Make forth. The Generals would have some words.
OCTAVIUS, ⌐*to his Officers*⌐   Stir not until the signal.
                    ⌐*The Generals step forward.*⌐
BRUTUS
Words before blows; is it so, countrymen?
OCTAVIUS
Not that we love words better, as you do.
BRUTUS
Good words are better than bad strokes, Octavius.   30
ANTONY
In your bad strokes, Brutus, you give good words.
Witness the hole you made in Caesar's heart,
Crying "Long live, hail, Caesar!"
CASSIUS   Antony,
The posture of your blows are yet unknown,   35
But, for your words, they rob the Hybla bees
And leave them honeyless.
ANTONY   Not stingless too.
BRUTUS   O yes, and soundless too,

44. **showed your teeth:** i.e., grinned
51. **might have ruled:** i.e., had had his way
52. **the cause:** the case at issue
53. **proof:** testing (of the argument) in battle
55. **goes up:** i.e., will be sheathed
57–58. **till . . . sword of traitors:** i.e., **till** I **(another Caesar)** also die on your swords
65. **peevish schoolboy:** i.e., Octavius
66. **masker . . . reveler:** i.e., Antony **masker:** one who indulges in masques, or disguisings

For you have stolen their buzzing, Antony,   40
And very wisely threat before you sting.
ANTONY
Villains, you did not so when your vile daggers
Hacked one another in the sides of Caesar.
You showed your ⌈teeth⌉ like apes and fawned like
    hounds   45
And bowed like bondmen, kissing Caesar's feet,
Whilst damnèd Casca, like a cur, behind
Struck Caesar on the neck. O you flatterers!
CASSIUS
Flatterers?—Now, Brutus, thank yourself!
This tongue had not offended so today   50
If Cassius might have ruled.
OCTAVIUS
Come, come, the cause. If arguing make us sweat,
The proof of it will turn to redder drops.
Look, I draw a sword against conspirators;
                                    ⌈*He draws.*⌉
When think you that the sword goes up again?   55
Never, till Caesar's three and thirty wounds
Be well avenged, or till another Caesar
Have added slaughter to the sword of traitors.
BRUTUS
Caesar, thou canst not die by traitors' hands
Unless thou bring'st them with thee.   60
OCTAVIUS   So I hope.
I was not born to die on Brutus' sword.
BRUTUS
O, if thou wert the noblest of thy strain,
Young man, thou couldst not die more honorable.
CASSIUS
A peevish schoolboy, worthless of such honor,   65
Joined with a masker and a reveler!
ANTONY
Old Cassius still.
OCTAVIUS   Come, Antony, away!—

71. **stomachs:** i.e., courage; or, inclination
72. **bark:** small sailing vessel
73. **on the hazard:** at stake
82. **set:** hazard
84. **held Epicurus strong:** believed strongly in the ideas of **Epicurus** (who denied supernatural influence on human affairs and, therefore, did not believe in omens)
86. **presage:** foretell
87. **former ensign:** foremost standard (See picture, below.)
90. **Who:** i.e., the eagles; **consorted:** accompanied
92. **kites:** birds of prey (See picture, page 180.)
94. **As:** as if

Roman ensign or standard. (5.1.87)
From Claude Paradin, *Deuises heroiques* . . . (1562).

Defiance, traitors, hurl we in your teeth.
If you dare fight today, come to the field;   70
If not, when you have stomachs.
                    Octavius, Antony, and ⌐their¬ army exit.
CASSIUS
Why now, blow wind, swell billow, and swim bark!
The storm is up, and all is on the hazard.
BRUTUS
Ho, Lucilius, hark, a word with you.
                    Lucilius and Messala stand forth.
LUCILIUS My lord?   75
                    ⌐*Brutus and Lucilius step aside together.*¬
CASSIUS
Messala.
MESSALA   What says my general?
CASSIUS   Messala,
This is my birthday, as this very day
Was Cassius born. Give me thy hand, Messala.   80
Be thou my witness that against my will
(As Pompey was) am I compelled to set
Upon one battle all our liberties.
You know that I held Epicurus strong
And his opinion. Now I change my mind   85
And partly credit things that do presage.
Coming from Sardis, on our former ensign
Two mighty eagles fell, and there they perched,
Gorging and feeding from our soldiers' hands,
Who to Philippi here consorted us.   90
This morning are they fled away and gone,
And in their steads do ravens, crows, and kites
Fly o'er our heads and downward look on us
As we were sickly prey. Their shadows seem
A canopy most fatal, under which   95
Our army lies, ready to give up the ghost.
MESSALA
Believe not so.

100. **constantly:** without wavering
103. **The gods:** i.e., may **the gods**
104. **Lovers:** friends
105. **rests still incertain:** remain always uncertain
111. **Cato:** See note to 2.1.318.
114. **fall:** befall, happen
114–15. **so to prevent / The time of life:** i.e., thus **to prevent** life's taking its natural course
116. **stay:** wait for
120. **Thorough:** through

CASSIUS   I but believe it partly,
For I am fresh of spirit and resolved
To meet all perils very constantly.   100
BRUTUS
Even so, Lucilius.   ⌜*Brutus returns to Cassius.*⌝
CASSIUS   Now, most noble Brutus,
The gods today stand friendly that we may,
Lovers in peace, lead on our days to age.
But since the affairs of men rests still incertain,   105
Let's reason with the worst that may befall.
If we do lose this battle, then is this
The very last time we shall speak together.
What are you then determinèd to do?
BRUTUS
Even by the rule of that philosophy   110
By which I did blame Cato for the death
Which he did give himself (I know not how,
But I do find it cowardly and vile,
For fear of what might fall, so to prevent
The time of life), arming myself with patience   115
To stay the providence of some high powers
That govern us below.
CASSIUS Then, if we lose this battle,
You are contented to be led in triumph
Thorough the streets of Rome?   120
BRUTUS
No, Cassius, no. Think not, thou noble Roman,
That ever Brutus will go bound to Rome.
He bears too great a mind. But this same day
Must end that work the ides of March begun.
And whether we shall meet again, I know not.   125
Therefore our everlasting farewell take.
Forever and forever farewell, Cassius.
If we do meet again, why we shall smile;
If not, why then this parting was well made.

5.2 Brutus sends Messala to throw all Brutus's legions into the battle.

___

0 SD. **Alarum:** a trumpet call to arms
1. **bills:** i.e., written instructions
4. **cold demeanor:** lack of spirit; **wing:** i.e., troops (literally, a military division placed to one side of the main body of an army)

5.3 Cassius, mistakenly believing that the battle has been lost and that Titinius has been taken captive, orders Pindarus to kill him. When Titinius returns, he puts his wreath of victory on Cassius's head and kills himself. Brutus orders his legions into battle again in order to conquer the still undefeated Antony.

___

1. **fly:** flee
2. **mine own:** i.e., my own men
3. **ensign:** standard-bearer
4. **it:** i.e., the standard (See picture, page 184.)

CASSIUS
Forever and forever farewell, Brutus.   130
If we do meet again, we'll smile indeed;
If not, 'tis true this parting was well made.
BRUTUS
Why then, lead on.—O, that a man might know
The end of this day's business ere it come!
But it sufficeth that the day will end,   135
And then the end is known.—Come ho, away!
They exit.

⌜Scene 2⌝

Alarum. Enter Brutus and Messala.

BRUTUS
Ride, ride, Messala, ride, and give these bills
Unto the legions on the other side!
⌜*He hands Messala papers.*⌝
Loud alarum.
Let them set on at once, for I perceive
But cold demeanor in Octavius' wing,
And sudden push gives them the overthrow.   5
Ride, ride, Messala! Let them all come down.
They exit.

⌜Scene 3⌝

*Alarums. Enter Cassius ⌜carrying a standard⌝ and
Titinius.*

CASSIUS
O, look, Titinius, look, the villains fly!
Myself have to mine own turned enemy.
This ensign here of mine was turning back;
I slew the coward and did take it from him.

7. **spoil:** looting

20. **even with a thought:** i.e., as quickly as **a thought**

22. **thick:** i.e., bad, weak

23. **thou not'st:** you observe

26. **is:** i.e., has; **run his compass:** ended its journey; completed its circle; finished its circuit of time

TITINIUS
O Cassius, Brutus gave the word too early,   5
Who, having some advantage on Octavius,
Took it too eagerly. His soldiers fell to spoil,
Whilst we by Antony are all enclosed.

Enter Pindarus.

PINDARUS
Fly further off, my lord, fly further off!
Mark Antony is in your tents, my lord.   10
Fly therefore, noble Cassius, fly far off.
CASSIUS
This hill is far enough.—Look, look, Titinius,
Are those my tents where I perceive the fire?
TITINIUS
They are, my lord.
CASSIUS   Titinius, if thou lovest me,   15
Mount thou my horse and hide thy spurs in him
Till he have brought thee up to yonder troops
And here again, that I may rest assured
Whether yond troops are friend or enemy.
TITINIUS
I will be here again even with a thought.   *He exits.*   20
CASSIUS
Go, Pindarus, get higher on that hill.
My sight was ever thick. Regard Titinius
And tell me what thou not'st about the field.
                       ⌐*Pindarus goes up.*⌐
This day I breathèd first. Time is come round,
And where I did begin, there shall I end;   25
My life is run his compass.—Sirrah, what news?
PINDARUS, *above.*   O my lord!
CASSIUS   What news?
PINDARUS
Titinius is enclosèd round about

30. **on the spur:** i.e., riding rapidly

32. **some light:** i.e., **some** soldiers alight, dismount

47. **hilts:** i.e., hilt of the sword

56. **change:** i.e., exchange of advantage

With horsemen that make to him on the spur,   30
Yet he spurs on. Now they are almost on him.
Now Titinius! Now some light. O, he lights too.
He's ta'en.   *Shout.*
          And hark, they shout for joy.
CASSIUS Come down, behold no more.—   35
O, coward that I am to live so long
To see my best friend ta'en before my face!
                              Pindarus ⌐comes down.¬
Come hither, sirrah.
In Parthia did I take thee prisoner,
And then I swore thee, saving of thy life,   40
That whatsoever I did bid thee do
Thou shouldst attempt it. Come now, keep thine
     oath.
Now be a freeman, and with this good sword,
That ran through Caesar's bowels, search this   45
     bosom.
Stand not to answer. Here, take thou the hilts,
And, when my face is covered, as 'tis now,
Guide thou the sword.   *⌐Pindarus stabs him.¬*
                    Caesar, thou art revenged   50
Even with the sword that killed thee.   *⌐He dies.¬*
PINDARUS
So I am free, yet would not so have been,
Durst I have done my will.—O Cassius!—
Far from this country Pindarus shall run,
Where never Roman shall take note of him.   55
                                     ⌐He exits.¬

          Enter Titinius and Messala.

MESSALA
   It is but change, Titinius, for Octavius
   Is overthrown by noble Brutus' power,
   As Cassius' legions are by Antony.

73. **Mistrust of my success:** i.e., fear about what had happened to me

74. **Mistrust of good success:** doubt as to the probability of a **good** outcome

76. **apt:** ready

79. **kill'st the mother:** i.e., destroys Melancholy, error's mother (by destroying the melancholy person) See picture, below.

Melancholy. (5.3.75)
From Cesare Ripa, *Iconologia* . . . (1611).

TITINIUS
These tidings will well comfort Cassius.
MESSALA
Where did you leave him?   60
TITINIUS   All disconsolate,
With Pindarus his bondman, on this hill.
MESSALA
Is not that he that lies upon the ground?
TITINIUS
He lies not like the living. O my heart!
MESSALA
Is not that he?   65
TITINIUS   No, this was he, Messala,
But Cassius is no more. O setting sun,
As in thy red rays thou dost sink to night,
So in his red blood Cassius' day is set.
The sun of Rome is set. Our day is gone;   70
Clouds, dews, and dangers come. Our deeds are
     done.
Mistrust of my success hath done this deed.
MESSALA
Mistrust of good success hath done this deed.
O hateful error, melancholy's child,   75
Why dost thou show to the apt thoughts of men
The things that are not? O error, soon conceived,
Thou never com'st unto a happy birth
But kill'st the mother that engendered thee!
TITINIUS
What, Pindarus! Where art thou, Pindarus?   80
MESSALA
Seek him, Titinius, whilst I go to meet
The noble Brutus, thrusting this report
Into his ears. I may say "thrusting it,"
For piercing steel and darts envenomèd
Shall be as welcome to the ears of Brutus   85
As tidings of this sight.

107. **own proper:** i.e., very **own**
109. **whe'er . . . not:** i.e., how he has   **whe'er:**
whether

"Wreath of victory." (5.3.91)
From Giacomo Lauri, *Antiquae vrbis splendor* . . . (1612–15).

TITINIUS　　　　　　　　　Hie you, Messala,
And I will seek for Pindarus the while.
　　　　　　　　　　　⌐*Messala exits.*⌐
Why didst thou send me forth, brave Cassius?
Did I not meet thy friends, and did not they　　　　　90
Put on my brows this wreath of victory
And bid me give it thee? Didst thou not hear their
　shouts?
Alas, thou hast misconstrued everything.
But hold thee, take this garland on thy brow.　　　　95
　　　　⌐*Laying the garland on Cassius' brow.*⌐
Thy Brutus bid me give it thee, and I
Will do his bidding.—Brutus, come apace,
And see how I regarded Caius Cassius.—
By your leave, gods, this is a Roman's part.
Come, Cassius' sword, and find Titinius' heart!　　　100
　　　　　　　⌐*He*⌐ *dies* ⌐*on Cassius' sword.*⌐

Alarum. Enter Brutus, Messala, young Cato, Strato,
　Volumnius, and Lucilius, ⌐*Labeo, and Flavius.*⌐

BRUTUS
　Where, where, Messala, doth his body lie?
MESSALA
　Lo, yonder, and Titinius mourning it.
BRUTUS
　Titinius' face is upward.
CATO　　　　　　　　　　He is slain.
BRUTUS
　O Julius Caesar, thou art mighty yet;　　　　　　105
　Thy spirit walks abroad and turns our swords
　In our own proper entrails.　　　　*Low alarums.*
CATO　　　　　　　　　　Brave Titinius!—
　Look whe'er he have not crowned dead Cassius.
BRUTUS
　Are yet two Romans living such as these?—　　　110
　The last of all the Romans, fare thee well.

117. **Thasos:** an island off the coast of Thrace, not far from Philippi

118. **funerals:** funeral

119. **discomfort us:** deprive us of courage, dishearten us

5.4 Brutus's forces are defeated in the second battle. Lucilius calls attention to himself and away from Brutus by announcing himself to be Brutus. Lucilius is captured, but Antony spares him.

---

4. **Marcus Cato:** See note to 2.1.318.

It is impossible that ever Rome
Should breed thy fellow.—Friends, I owe more
    tears
To this dead man than you shall see me pay.—   115
I shall find time, Cassius; I shall find time.—
Come, therefore, and to ⌐Thasos⌐ send his body.
His funerals shall not be in our camp,
Lest it discomfort us.—Lucilius, come.—
And come, young Cato. Let us to the field.—   120
Labeo and Flavius, set our battles on.
'Tis three o'clock, and, Romans, yet ere night
We shall try fortune in a second fight.

                                    They exit.

                    ⌐Scene 4⌐

Alarum. Enter Brutus, Messala, Cato, Lucilius, and
                    Flavius.

BRUTUS
Yet, countrymen, O, yet hold up your heads!
            ⌐*Brutus, Messala, and Flavius exit.*⌐
CATO
What bastard doth not? Who will go with me?
I will proclaim my name about the field.
I am the son of Marcus Cato, ho!
A foe to tyrants and my country's friend.   5
I am the son of Marcus Cato, ho!

            Enter Soldiers and fight.

⌐LUCILIUS⌐
And I am Brutus, Marcus Brutus, I!
Brutus, my country's friend! Know me for Brutus.
                        ⌐*Cato is killed.*⌐
O young and noble Cato, art thou down?

13. **Only I yield:** i.e., **I yield only**
14. **so much:** i.e., this **much** money; **straight:** immediately
25. **or . . . or:** either . . . **or**

Why, now thou diest as bravely as Titinius   10
And mayst be honored, being Cato's son.
⌜FIRST⌝ SOLDIER, ⌜*seizing Lucilius*⌝
    Yield, or thou diest.
LUCILIUS   Only I yield to die.
There is so much that thou wilt kill me straight.
                                ⌜*Offering money.*⌝
Kill Brutus and be honored in his death.   15
⌜FIRST⌝ SOLDIER
    We must not. A noble prisoner!

                    Enter Antony.

SECOND SOLDIER
    Room, ho! Tell Antony Brutus is ta'en.
FIRST SOLDIER
    I'll tell ⌜the⌝ news. Here comes the General.—
    Brutus is ta'en, Brutus is ta'en, my lord.
ANTONY Where is he?   20
LUCILIUS
    Safe, Antony, Brutus is safe enough.
    I dare assure thee that no enemy
    Shall ever take alive the noble Brutus.
    The gods defend him from so great a shame!
    When you do find him, or alive or dead,   25
    He will be found like Brutus, like himself.
ANTONY
    This is not Brutus, friend, but I assure you,
    A prize no less in worth. Keep this man safe.
    Give him all kindness. I had rather have
    Such men my friends than enemies. Go on,   30
    And see whe'er Brutus be alive or dead,
    And bring us word unto Octavius' tent
    How everything is chanced.
                    They exit ⌜in different directions.⌝

5.5 Brutus begs four of his followers to assist him in his suicide. All but the fourth decline. Brutus kills himself. Antony praises Brutus as the only honorable conspirator, and Octavius orders Brutus's funeral rites.

---

1. **remains:** remainder, those remaining from a larger number
2. **showed the torchlight:** i.e., signaled back
3. **or ta'en:** either taken
13. **ill:** harsh; painful; evil
14. **meditates:** deliberates
17. **List:** listen to, pay attention to

⌐Scene 5⌐

Enter Brutus, Dardanus, Clitus, Strato, and Volumnius.

BRUTUS
  Come, poor remains of friends, rest on this rock.
                                    ⌐*He sits down.*⌐
CLITUS
  Statilius showed the torchlight, but, my lord,
  He came not back. He is or ta'en or slain.
BRUTUS
  Sit thee down, Clitus. Slaying is the word;
  It is a deed in fashion. Hark thee, Clitus.   5
                                    ⌐*He whispers to Clitus.*⌐
CLITUS
  What, I, my lord? No, not for all the world.
BRUTUS
  Peace, then, no words.
CLITUS   I'll rather kill myself.
BRUTUS
  Hark thee, Dardanus.   ⌐*He whispers to Dardanus.*⌐
DARDANUS   Shall I do such a deed?   10
CLITUS   O Dardanus!
DARDANUS   O Clitus!
                          ⌐*Dardanus and Clitus step aside.*⌐
CLITUS
  What ill request did Brutus make to thee?
DARDANUS
  To kill him, Clitus. Look, he meditates.
CLITUS
  Now is that noble vessel full of grief,   15
  That it runs over even at his eyes.
BRUTUS
  Come hither, good Volumnius. List a word.
VOLUMNIUS
  What says my lord?
BRUTUS   Why this, Volumnius:

21. **several:** separate; **Sardis:** See note to 4.2.31.

27. **beat us to the pit:** driven us, like wild animals, to the edge of a **pit** (The idea of "**pit**" as "grave" may also be present.)

31. **that our love:** i.e., **our love**

The ghost of Caesar hath appeared to me   20
Two several times by night—at Sardis once
And this last night here in Philippi fields.
I know my hour is come.
VOLUMNIUS   Not so, my lord.
BRUTUS
Nay, I am sure it is, Volumnius.   25
Thou seest the world, Volumnius, how it goes.
Our enemies have beat us to the pit.   *Low alarums.*
It is more worthy to leap in ourselves
Than tarry till they push us. Good Volumnius,
Thou know'st that we two went to school together;   30
Even for that our love of old, I prithee,
Hold thou my sword hilts whilst I run on it.
VOLUMNIUS
That's not an office for a friend, my lord.
                              Alarum ⌜continues.⌝
CLITUS
Fly, fly, my lord! There is no tarrying here.
BRUTUS
Farewell to you—and you—and you, Volumnius.—   35
Strato, thou hast been all this while asleep.
Farewell to thee, too, Strato.—Countrymen,
My heart doth joy that yet in all my life
I found no man but he was true to me.
I shall have glory by this losing day   40
More than Octavius and Mark Antony
By this vile conquest shall attain unto.
So fare you well at once, for Brutus' tongue
Hath almost ended his life's history.
Night hangs upon mine eyes; my bones would rest,   45
That have but labored to attain this hour.
                    Alarum. Cry within "Fly, fly, fly!"
CLITUS
Fly, my lord, fly!
BRUTUS   Hence. I will follow.
                  ⌜All exit but Brutus and Strato.⌝

51. **smatch:** taste
57 SD. **Retreat:** signal to retreat or withdraw
62. **only:** alone
65. **saying:** assertion (See 5.4.22–26, above.)
66. **entertain them:** i.e., take them into my service
68. **prefer:** recommend

A sixteenth-century image of Brutus's suicide.
From Geoffrey Whitney, *A choice of emblemes* . . . (1586).

I prithee, Strato, stay thou by thy lord.
Thou art a fellow of a good respect;   50
Thy life hath had some smatch of honor in it.
Hold, then, my sword, and turn away thy face
While I do run upon it. Wilt thou, Strato?

STRATO
Give me your hand first. Fare you well, my lord.

BRUTUS
Farewell, good Strato.   55
              ⌈*Brutus runs on his sword.*⌉
Caesar, now be still.
I killed not thee with half so good a will.   ⌈*He*⌉ *dies.*

Alarum. Retreat. Enter Antony, Octavius, Messala,
Lucilius, and the army.

OCTAVIUS   What man is that?

MESSALA
My master's man.—Strato, where is thy master?

STRATO
Free from the bondage you are in, Messala.   60
The conquerors can but make a fire of him,
For Brutus only overcame himself,
And no man else hath honor by his death.

LUCILIUS
So Brutus should be found.—I thank thee, Brutus,
That thou hast proved Lucilius' saying true.   65

OCTAVIUS
All that served Brutus, I will entertain them.—
Fellow, wilt thou bestow thy time with me?

STRATO
Ay, if Messala will prefer me to you.

OCTAVIUS
Do so, good Messala.

MESSALA   How died my master, Strato?   70

STRATO
I held the sword, and he did run on it.

73. **latest:** final
76. **envy of:** malice toward
77. **only:** alone
78. **made one of:** joined
79. **gentle:** noble
82. **virtue:** probably the Roman *virtus*, manly excellence
85. **ordered honorably:** treated with honor
86. **field:** i.e., army in **the field**
87. **part:** share; **happy:** fortunate

MESSALA
Octavius, then take him to follow thee,
That did the latest service to my master.
ANTONY
This was the noblest Roman of them all.
All the conspirators save only he   75
Did that they did in envy of great Caesar.
He only in a general honest thought
And common good to all made one of them.
His life was gentle and the elements
So mixed in him that nature might stand up   80
And say to all the world "This was a man."
OCTAVIUS
According to his virtue, let us use him
With all respect and rites of burial.
Within my tent his bones tonight shall lie,
Most like a soldier, ordered honorably.   85
So call the field to rest, and let's away
To part the glories of this happy day.
                                                             They all exit.

Textual Notes

The reading of the present text appears to the left of the bracket. The earliest sources of readings not in **F,** the First Folio text (upon which this edition is based), are indicated as follows: **F2** is the Second Folio of 1632; **F3** is the Third Folio of 1663–64; **F4** is the Fourth Folio of 1685; **Q (1691)** is the quarto of 1691; **Ed.** is an earlier editor of Shakespeare, beginning with Rowe in 1709. No sources are given for emendations of punctuation or for corrections of obvious typographical errors, like turned letters that produce no known word. Other symbols: **SD** means stage direction; **SP** means speech prefix; *uncorr.* means the first or uncorrected state of the First Folio; *corr.* means the second or corrected state of the First Folio; ~ stands in place of a word already quoted before the bracket; ∧ indicates the omission of a punctuation mark.

1.1	42. Pompey? . . . oft∧] ~∧ . . . ~? F
	44. windows,] ~? F
	58. your] F *corr.;* yonr F *uncorr.*
1.2	29. SD *Brutus and Cassius*] F (*Brut. & Cass.*)
	152. yours?] ~∧ F
	175. not, so∧] ~ ∧~ (F
	265. like;] ~∧ F
1.3	113. offal∧] ~? F
	134. In] Ed.; Is F
2.1	14. question.] ~? F
	24. climber-upward] ~∧~ F
	42. ides] Ed.; first F
	70. of man] F2; of a man F
	110. SD *Brutus . . . Cassius*] Ed.; *They* F
	133. women,] ~. F

211

147. oath,] ~. F
191. envious;] ~. F
230. eighth] F (eight)
247. SD *All . . . exit.*] F (*Exeunt. Manet Brutus.*)
274. condition] Condltion F
275. Brutus] *Brntus* F
287. his] F2; hit F
295. half,] ~ʌ F
302. the] F2; tho F
334. SD *1 line earlier in* F
339 *to the end of scene.* SP LIGARIUS] Ed.;
    Cai. F

2.2   19. fought] Ed.; fight F
23. did] F2; do F
49. are] Ed.; heare F
2.3   1. SP ARTEMIDORUS] Ed.; *omit* F
3.1   0. SD *Enter . . . Petitioners.*] This ed.; *Enter*
    Caesar, Brutus, Cassius, Caska, Decius,
    Metellus, Trebonius, Cynna, Antony,
    Lepidus, Artimedorus, Publius, and the
    Soothsayer. F
43. law] Ed.; lane F
84. SD *As . . . Caesar.*] This ed.; *They stab*
    Caesar. F
126. states] F2; State F
128. lies] F2; lye F
184. And] F *corr.;* A nd F *uncorr.*
202. First] Flrst F
217. foes—] ~? F
218. noble!— . . . corpse?] ~, . . . ~, F
279. SD *All . . . exit.*] F (*Exeunt. Manet Antony.*)
280. SP ANTONY] Q (1691); *omit* F
309. catching, for] F2; catchingʌ from F
3.2   0. SD *Enter . . . Cassius*] Ed.; *Enter Brutus*
    and goes into the Pulpit, and Cassius F
1. SP PLEBEIANS] Ed.; *Ple.* F
7, 11. renderèd] Ed.; rendred F

37, 50, 81, 151, 166, 173, 180, 244, 248, 253, 260. SP PLEBEIANS] Ed.; *All.* F
37. Brutus] *Btutus* F
70, 160. SP PLEBEIANS] This ed.; *omit* F
114. art] F2; are F
216. SP PLEBEIANS] Ed.; *omit* F
233. wit] F2; writ F
276. SD *1 line later in* F

4.2 1. Stand] F *corr.;* Srand F *uncorr.*
38. SP FIRST SOLDIER] Ed.; *omit* F
39. SP SECOND SOLDIER] Ed.; *omit* F
40. SP THIRD SOLDIER] Ed.; *omit* F
56. Lucius] Ed.; *Lucillius* F
58. Lucilius] Ed.; *Lucius* F
58. SD *All . . . exit.*] F (*Exeunt. Manet Brutus and Cassius.*)

4.3 131. ill-tempered] ill remper'd F
182. SD *Lucius*] Ed.; *Boy* F
244. besides] F (beside)
248. to] ro F
264. SD *1 line earlier in* F
277. SD *All . . . exit.*] Ed.; *Exeunt.* F
291. will not] F2; will it not F
309. slumber] slumbler F
317. SD *1 line earlier in* F
339. Lucius] *Lucus* F

5.1 44. teeth] F3; teethes F
92. steads] F (steeds)

5.3 37. SD *Pindarus comes down.*] Ed.; *Enter Pindarus.* F
80. Pindarus?] F *corr.;* ~. F *uncorr.*
109. have not crowned] F *corr.* (haue not crown'd); haue crown'd F *uncorr.*
113. more] F *corr.* (mo); no F *uncorr.*
117. Thasos] Ed.; *Tharsus* F

5.4 4. Marcus] F *corr.;* Marcns F *uncorr.*
7. SP LUCILIUS] Ed.; *omit* F

9. O] Ed.; *Luc.* O F
18. the news] Ed.; thee newes F
20. he] F *corr.* (hee); kee F *uncorr.*
5.5   27. SD *Low*] F *corr.; Loud* F *uncorr.*
33. SD *continues*] This ed.; *still* F

Julius Caesar:
A Modern Perspective

Coppélia Kahn

When Cassius tries to persuade his friend Brutus that they must halt Julius Caesar's rise to power, Cassius speaks of an idealized "Rome" of the past in which kingship was unthinkable:

> Rome, thou hast lost the breed of noble bloods! . . .
> O, you and I have heard our fathers say
> There was a Brutus once that would have brooked
> Th' eternal devil to keep his state in Rome
> As easily as a king.   (1.2.160, 167–70)

A few scenes later (2.1), Brutus wrestles with the question of whether Caesar intends to become king, and recalls his own namesake:

> My ancestors did from the streets of Rome
> The Tarquin drive when he was called a king.
>   (2.1.56–57)

As many in Shakespeare's audience might have known, Rome began as a kingship that lasted some 150 years until Lucius Junius Brutus, ancestor of this play's Brutus, led an uprising in 510 B.C.E. that drove the reigning dynasty from Rome, abolished kingship itself, and established the Roman Republic. Both Cassius and Brutus equate Rome with the Republic and the values it purports to embody. They see themselves as Romans because they believe in the Republic and because they

215

repudiate kingship so that power can be shared among the elected rulers, the aristocratic patricians who make up the Senate, and the people. Then, supposedly, no one man can dominate Rome; all male citizens will be free, and equal. (The government of the United States, in which power is shared among the president, the Congress, and the Supreme Court, is modeled on the Roman Republic, and the pledge of allegiance to the flag mentions "the republic . . . with liberty and justice for all.") Brutus, once he is convinced that Caesar "would be crowned," sees himself as destined to repeat his ancestor's heroic mission: by killing Caesar, he will, he thinks, restore the true "Rome"—the Republic.

The Roman Republic, however, never existed in the pure form in which the conspirators imagine it, and the reign of terror unleashed by their assassination of Caesar gave rise precisely to the rule of "one man" that they hoped to prevent. Octavius Caesar became sole emperor of Rome by defeating the conspirators in the final battle at Philippi in 42 B.C.E. and then by conquering his former ally Antony at Actium in 31 B.C.E. This is the play's tragic irony, and some knowledge of Roman history can help us to appreciate it.

In the century or so preceding the assassination of Julius Caesar in 44 B.C.E., the Roman Republic endured almost constant upheavals. The reforms in land ownership introduced between 134 and 122 B.C.E. provoked fierce resistance from the patrician class, and those who introduced the reforms were killed after armed battles between their followers and those defending the Senate. The senators regained power for a time, but then two rival generals, Marius, in 107 B.C.E., and Sulla, in 88 B.C.E., took control. Each with his massive armies occupied Rome; each carried out a reign of terror—largely under republican law—in which his political opponents were openly slaughtered.

Next came Pompey, who acquired the surname *Magnus,* meaning "the great," by helping Sulla destroy Marius. (In the play's first scene, the tribunes recall Pompey as Julius Caesar's predecessor.) Granted extraordinary powers by the Senate, Pompey swept the Mediterranean clean of pirates and defeated Mithradates VI, king of Pontus, making himself in effect the uncrowned emperor of Rome's eastern provinces. Locked in rivalry with Julius Caesar, who defeated him at Pharsalus in 48 B.C.E., Pompey held more power and authority than any one man in Rome had ever had. The Republic never, for more than brief periods, functioned as it was supposed to—as a combination of monarchy (in the consuls), oligarchy (in the Senate), and democracy that, by keeping all three forms of power in balance, would prevent the worst tendencies of each. Instead, the Republic fostered the division of the aristocracy into factions and the rise of military superheroes whose armies were loyal to them rather than to the Republic.

The republican ideal that Cassius evokes to seduce Brutus into opposing Caesar, and that Brutus uses to justify murder, is closer to myth than to history (though it was also dearly cherished as an ideal even during the worst conflicts of the republican era). Or we might call it an ideology, which, according to Louis Althusser, is a set of imagined relations as opposed to the actual political conditions of Rome. Cassius correctly assumes that Brutus shares this ideology. As "noble bloods" of the ruling elite, both Cassius and Brutus believe themselves to have earned their reputations as "honorable men" by serving the state. That Caesar, one of their own class, has outstripped them in the ordinary course of advancement through state offices (the *cursus honorum,* or "racetrack" of honors) is an affront to their honor as Romans. Of course, Brutus and Cassius differ in character: Brutus wouldn't stoop to the deception Cassius practices by planting in Brutus's study faked petitions from citizens supposedly clamoring for Brutus to topple Caesar. And it wouldn't occur to Cassius to justify Caesar's murder by calling it "a sacrifice." Yet they are equally blinded to the complex politics of Rome by their shared republican mentality. *Julius Caesar* has often been treated almost as a set of individual character studies. And it is true that Shakespeare's "noble Romans" are vividly differentiated. However, they are all conceived within and motivated by a common sense of class identity as patricians and of national identity as Romans defending the Republic.

While Brutus and Cassius ponder their loss of status as Caesar's "underlings" (1.2.148), within earshot a crowd roars for him. Though in person Caesar may fall short of the mystique he generates, he knows how to inspire massive public approval. In contrast, for Brutus and Cassius the people hardly exist. Casca's account of how Caesar refused the crown drips with aristocratic disdain for the "tag-rag people." Yet why, according to him, did the people cheer for Caesar?

> . . . still as he refused [the crown] the rabblement hooted and clapped their chopped hands and threw up their sweaty nightcaps and uttered such a deal of stinking breath because Caesar refused the crown. . . . (1.2.254–58)

Seemingly, the people too are captive to the republican ideal. Then Brutus's fear that "the people / Choose Caesar for their king" must be mistaken. Or is it? For when Caesar "perceived the common herd was glad he refused the crown, he plucked . . . ope his doublet and offered them his throat to cut" (1.2.274–77). He is obviously playing to the grandstands, in what amounts to a parody of serving "the general good," in order to milk the crowd's adoration. But does it lie within the people's power to confer the crown? Evidently not, for it is Antony who offers it, and in the next scene Casca says "the Senators tomorrow / Mean to establish Caesar as a king" (1.3.88–89). The patricians, then, are divided into factions for and against Caesar. But is any faction strong enough to override the people's will? As Antony's funeral oration demonstrates, the man who can convince the masses that Caesar—in high republican fashion—was devoted to *them* can rule Rome. Thus it would appear that republican ideology can be successfully co-opted by ambitious men like Caesar and Antony. While grasping power for their own interests, they convince those who give it to them that they use it only for "the general good"—thus establishing a set of imagined social relations that masks the real ones.

Brutus sets out to kill Caesar in the conviction that Caesar "would be crowned." The glimpses of Caesar that Shakespeare allows us neither confirm nor refute this belief. Grandiose but physically infirm, imperious but easily manipulated by flattery, in his last moments he resembles the Caesar of Casca's account who loves to delude himself and others into thinking that he embodies the selfless, constant servant of the state. "What touches us ourself shall be last served," he declares (3.1.8), and, refusing entreaties, continues:

> But I am constant as the Northern Star,
> Of whose true fixed and resting quality
> There is no fellow in the firmament. . . .
> Let me a little show it, even in this:
> That I was constant Cimber should be banished
> And constant do remain to keep him so.
> (3.1.66–68, 77–79)

Disturbingly, it is Brutus who most resembles Caesar in playing the republican role. Both Caesar and Brutus are self-conscious about their particular virtues and concerned to display them publicly, no matter what their actual feelings. Caesar wants to be known for his courage. Warning Antony that Cassius's envy is dangerous, he says, "I rather tell thee what is to be feared / Than what I fear; for always I am Caesar" (1.2.221–22). Alone with his wife, who urges him to heed the portents of disaster and stay home from the Capitol, he speaks of himself in the same ringing tones that mark his public utterance: "Caesar shall forth. The things that threatened me / Ne'er looked but on my back" (2.2.10–11). Brutus, quite similarly, takes pains to make public the moral principles behind his actions. When he is alone, he calls the prospect of murdering Caesar "a dreadful thing" and refers to the "monstrous visage" of conspiracy (2.1.66, 88). But once the conspiracy gathers, he refers only to the "virtue of our enterprise" (2.1.144).

As if to underline similarities between these two adversaries, Shakespeare parallels them in two successive scenes, 2.1. and 2.2. Both characters are shown as uneasy and unable to sleep; both greet the same group of men, shaking hands and naming them: to Brutus, they are fellow conspirators; to Caesar, "good friends." Each, making a fatally wrong decision, reveals his vanity. Brutus refuses to allow Mark Antony to be killed as well as Caesar because it would make the deed "too bloody," then rationalizes the inherent, unavoidable bloodiness of murder into a pious, ceremonial sacrifice, "necessary and not envious [i.e., malicious]" (2.1.175–96). Caesar decides to go to the Capitol despite Calphurnia's warning and allows Decius to flatter him that her dream of his statue running blood symbolizes his miraculous ability to revive Rome (2.2.88–95).

Finally, as Norman Rabkin has noted, Shakespeare presents each character alone with his wife, responding to her suspicion that he is facing some danger. (See Further Reading, page 235.) In his other plays based on Roman history, Shakespeare gives women much more prominence than in *Julius Caesar,* where Portia and Calphurnia each speak in only two scenes. In this play Rome is more intensely a man's world than in Shakespeare's main sources, Plutarch's biographies of Caesar, Brutus, and Mark Antony. While Plutarch notes the intermarriages among patricians that held their political alliances together and recounts with relish anecdotes in which women figure prominently, Shakespeare focuses dramatic interest on relations among men. Indeed, in terms of the Republic, to be a Roman means to be gendered male. Our word "virtue" comes from the Latin word *virtus,* meaning both manliness and valor, which is derived from Latin *vir,* man. The virtues promoted by the social and political life of the Republic are also gendered masculine and considered proper to men alone, as is made clear in the two scenes in which Portia is onstage.

In the first, when Portia begs Brutus to "tell me your counsels," she asks not for specific information about the conspiracy so much as for intimacy, a sharing of thoughts and feelings based on mutual trust. What keeps Brutus from trusting her is that she is a woman and, according to gender conventions that survive even today, considered incapable of self-restraint and prone to telling secrets. (Brutus refers to the conspirators as "secret Romans that will not palter"—will not shift position and thus divulge the conspiracy.) But Brutus's Romanness, which is virtually the same as his masculinity, also inhibits him from revealing inner conflict, self-doubt, or vulnerability to anyone, male or female. Portia is as convinced as Brutus that only those who show masculine valor deserve trust, and so she tries to cross the gender barrier by giving herself "a voluntary wound" in the thigh, a simulation of the battle wounds men customarily incurred in defending the Republic, wounds that earned them honor and political office. Though we can infer from her anxiety in 2.4 that Brutus has told her of the conspiracy, that scene indicates her doubts about sustaining the masculine virtue toward which she has aspired, and it shows her reversion to an image of herself as necessarily fearful and untrustworthy because she is a woman: "How hard it is for women to keep counsel! . . . / Ay me, how weak a thing / The heart of woman is!" (2.4.10, 45–46).

The politics of gender in *Julius Caesar* is governed by relations among men, however, rather than between men and women. Male friendships are indistinguishable from politics itself, from which women are formally excluded, and such friendships are strongly marked by rivalry. Pompey and Caesar were political allies before they became enemies; Brutus, though favored by Caesar, plots to kill him; Brutus and Cassius, bound by shared ideals, quarrel bitterly. Cassius's story of his swimming match with Caesar captures the routine intensity of competition that is central to the formation of men as Romans:

> For once, upon a raw and gusty day,
> The troubled Tiber chafing with her shores,
> Caesar said to me "Dar'st thou, Cassius, now
> Leap in with me into this angry flood
> And swim to yonder point?" Upon the word,
> Accoutered as I was, I plungèd in
> And bade him follow; so indeed he did.
> The torrent roared, and we did buffet it
> With lusty sinews, throwing it aside
> And stemming it with hearts of controversy.
> (1.2.107–16)

At a key moment in the play, when Brutus tries to justify murdering Caesar, he too evokes the rivalrous world of Roman politics:

> . . . lowliness is young ambition's ladder,
> Whereto the climber-upward turns his face;
> But, when he once attains the upmost round,
> He then unto the ladder turns his back,
> Looks in the clouds, scorning the base degrees
> By which he did ascend.
>
> (2.1.23–28)

Because Caesar has gained this "upmost round" and towers "like a Colossus" (1.2.143) above his former peers, they feel their manliness diminished. Cassius laments that "we are governed with our mothers' spirits. / Our yoke and sufferance show us womanish" (1.3.86–87). In raising their daggers against Caesar, then, they assert their manliness as Romans, and by bringing Caesar down and making him bleed, reduce him, as Gail Paster has shown, to the inferior status of a woman. (See Further Reading, page 234.)

Brutus persuades himself and the other conspirators that they can dissociate Caesar's spirit from his body, and wishes that it were possible to cut off Caesar's ambition without making him bleed for it. From the assassination scene to the end, however, Caesar's blood and corpse become key images in the contest for power between the conspirators and their opponents. Brutus urges his friends to bathe their hands in Caesar's blood as a sign of "Peace, freedom, and liberty" (3.1.118–22)—the death of a tyrant, the restoration of the Republic. But their opponent Mark Antony cleverly turns their gesture to his own advantage when he plucks the bloody mantle from Caesar's corpse to show the crowd his wounds and "let slip the dogs of war" (299)—*Mark Antony*'s war against Brutus and Cassius.

It is he who defeats them, through superior military tactics, in the final battle of Philippi, at which both conspirators take their own lives.

Earlier, Brutus had confessed to Cassius that he would commit suicide rather than "be led in triumph / Thorough [i.e., through] the streets of Rome" (5.1.119–20). And Cassius considers it dishonorable to live after he thinks he sees Titinius taken captive. Yet both imply in their last words that Caesar's spirit has taken revenge on them, and many critics have adopted this interpretation, which provides a certain kind of moral closure typical of Elizabethan revenge plays. But we need not seek explanations only in the supernatural realm. Brutus and Cassius, in effect, help to bring about their own downfall through their moral blindnesses and tactical errors, and Mark Antony foments civil war to serve his own interests. Curiously, the "monstrous apparition" that appears to Brutus in his tent on the eve of battle calls itself not Caesar but "Thy evil spirit" and says only "thou shalt see me at Philippi" (4.3.320, 325, 327). Perhaps Shakespeare is implying that Brutus's own fatal error of judgment in thinking that republican liberty could be achieved only by killing Caesar has resulted, quite contrary to his intentions, in evil. Brutus himself is not evil, though his uncompromising idealism carries with it a subtle vanity. We might say that he only carries to a misguided extreme the values and expectations implied in the republican ideals he inherited. As Cicero states, ". . . men may construe things after their fashion, / Clean from the purpose of the things themselves" (1.3.34–35).

Further Reading

Julius Caesar

Blits, Jan H. "Manliness and Friendship in Shakespeare's *Julius Caesar.*" *Interpretation* 9 (1980–81): 155–67.

Blits abstracts from Shakespeare's *Julius Caesar* a binary construction of gender by examining Portia, on the one hand, and the principal male characters, on the other. "The manly is associated with the firm, the brilliant, the cold, the independent, the high and the noble; the womanish, with the soft, the dull, the warm, the dependent, the low and the lowly." To achieve manliness, Caesar, Brutus, and Cassius all seek to acquire love from other men because "being loved closely resembles being honored. Both are tributes of esteem." The man who is the object of another man's love has succeeded in unmanning his friend by reducing him to the shamefully womanish: "Rome's civil strife seems to be Roman friendship writ large." Antony, for Blits, is a striking exception to this rule about Roman friendship insofar as Antony loves Caesar without either fearing domination by him, as do Cassius and Brutus, or desiring anything from him. Instead, Antony is willing to give up everything and destroy everything to demonstrate his love by avenging Caesar's death. Brutus and Cassius, though, conform, for Blits, to his rule about Roman friendship. Cassius is reduced to a womanish state by Brutus in the course of their reconciliation as friends following their quarrel (4.3). As Brutus is about to commit suicide, he finds "joy" in his "heart" that he has "found no man but . . . was true to" him (5.5.38–39), thereby having always prevailed in the Roman contest of friendship, although at the cost of being able ever to reciprocate offered love—not even the love of Portia, exhibited in her unsatisfied conjugal plea for intimacy.

Burckhardt, Sigurd. "How Not to Murder Caesar." In *Shakespearean Meanings*, pp. 3–21. Princeton, N.J.: Princeton University Press, 1968.

Making reference to Cassius's characterization of the assassination of Caesar as a "lofty scene [i.e., play or drama]" that shall "be acted over / In states unborn and accents yet unknown" (3.1.125–26), Burckhardt invites his readers to imagine Brutus and Cassius as the "authors" or "plotters" of the assassination as a drama and to pay attention to the style of the play they desire to create. Brutus takes charge of the style and intends to stage "not a bare assassination, but a tragedy of classical, almost Aristotelian, purity. There is to be no wholesale slaughter. . . . Only the tragic hero is to be killed, and the killing itself is to be a ritual, a sacrifice, formal and even beautiful." The "disastrous consequences" of the assassination then result from Brutus's mistaken assumptions about the audience for whom the tragedy is intended. Brutus supposes his audience to be "noble, sturdy republicans, capable of the moral discrimination and public spirit which classical tragedy demands." Instead the audience, as the play's first scene has already established, are "eager to be led, easily tricked, crude in their responses."

Bushnell, Rebecca W. "*Julius Caesar*." In *Companion to Shakespeare's Works*, edited by Richard Dutton and Jean E. Howard, 1:339–56. Malden, Mass.: Blackwell, 2003.

Bushnell resists the pressure to read *Julius Caesar* as a "seamless action and single political statement," advocating instead an approach that underscores its discontinuities of "political rhetoric, vocabulary, and ideologies." The fragmentation, anachronisms, and inconsistencies that earlier critics regarded as flaws reflect the play's political incoherence and "contribute to [its] uncanny power to undermine any ideological certainty." The drama's political resonance emanates from the sociocultural flux of the Tudor world in the middle of the sixteenth century, when "institutions, traditions, and languages of court, city, and regions coexisted and often conflicted, and political and social identities changed rapidly." Terms such as "tyranny," "liberty," "commons," and "commonwealth" became "watchwords" of a new political temper. Attending to the play's fractured nature "as an urban drama and a drama of state, a play of republican values and Tudor morality, and a play of two places—Rome and London," Bushnell concludes that *Julius Caesar* is a "dynamic political text" rather than "a classical monument or a tired classic."

Cicero, Marcus Tullius. "The Second Philippic of Marcus Tullius Cicero against Marcus Antonius." In *Cicero, Philippics*, trans. W. C. A. Ker, pp. 61–183. Loeb Classical Library. Cambridge, Mass.: Harvard University Press, 1926.

Cicero's second philippic, or oration, against Marcus Antonius (Shakespeare's Mark Antony) was composed in October of 44 B.C.E. both as a reply to Antonius's charges against Cicero and as an attack on Antonius. As the latter it is comprehensive, itemizing the immorality and criminality of Antonius both as a private citizen (beginning with his boyhood) and as a public and military official. At the same time the oration's language indicates how, only a few months after Caesar's assassination in the preceding March, his assassins were already being represented in the most extreme terms: "they, if they are not the liberators of the Roman people and the saviors of the State, are worse than assassins, worse than murderers, worse even than parricides—if indeed it be more atrocious to slay the father of the country than one's own." Cicero is forthright in his own approval of the assassination: "Is there then any man, except those that were glad of his [i.e., Caesar's] reign, who repudiated that deed, or disapproved of it when it was done? All therefore are to be blamed, for all good men, so far as their own power went, slew Caesar; some lacked a plan, others courage, others opportunity: will no man lacked." Although never delivered as a speech to the Roman Senate, the second philippic was published in November, 44 B.C.E. On 7 December 43 B.C.E. Cicero was murdered at Antonius's directive.

Greene, Gayle. " 'The Power of Speech to Stir Men's Blood': The Language of Tragedy in Shakespeare's *Julius Caesar*." *Renaissance Drama* 11 (1980): 67–93.

　　Positing that *Julius Caesar* as a whole is structured around a series of persuasion scenes, Greene suggests that a character's ability to wield words determines his or her fate. From this position Greene moves to uncover an "implied . . . criticism of rhetoric and language itself" within Shakespeare's depiction of Rome as a "society of skilled speakers." She discusses three such persuasion scenes: "the scene in which Cassius 'seduces' Brutus to come into the conspiracy [1.2.30–187]; the soliloquy in which Brutus 'fashions' an argument for himself to join the conspiracy [2.1.10–36]; and the forum scene, where first Brutus [3.2.14–42], then Antony [82–266], 'move' the crowd." In none of these, despite the success of the persuasion, does she find substantial grounds for their persuasiveness—no evidence for the charge of ambition laid against Cae-

sar by the conspirators, no justification for his assassination, no reason for the Roman populace to avenge
themselves on the conspirators. Addressing Brutus
in 1.2, Cassius seems to evoke honor and the general
good, but succeeds by appealing to Brutus's vanity. In
soliloquy, Brutus does not reason with himself, but lets
"words do his thinking for him." In Brutus's oration to
the Romans following the assassination, he provides
"no argument that could appeal to logic." And, finally,
Antony succeeds in turning the Romans into a vengeful
mob "by twisting a few crucial words."

Hadfield, Andrew. "The End of the Republic: *Titus
Andronicus* and *Julius Caesar.*" Chapter 5 in *Shake-
speare and Republicanism*, pp. 154–83, esp. pp. 167–83.
Cambridge: Cambridge University Press, 2005.

Beginning with the premise that "republicanism" is
"one of the key problems that defined [Shakespeare's]
working career," Hadfield reads *Julius Caesar* as a work
"designed to intervene in the political debates" of a
culture "saturated with republican images and argu-
ments." In the final decades of the Elizabethan era,
"republicanism" was more a "cluster of ideas" relating
to citizenship, friendship, natural rights, public virtue,
and a rhetoric against tyranny than a "monolithic concept indicating the participation of all citizens in the
political process." Hadfield rejects the "critical cliché"
that the real hero of the Roman plays is Rome and
argues instead that, like *Titus Andronicus, Julius Caesar* "depicts a dying and perverted republican Rome
that has lost the ability to inspire its citizens to behave
virtuously," without which ability the republic "cannot
function as a political force." Central to Hadfield's reading are Cicero's *De Officiis (Of Duties)* and *De Amicitia
(Of Friendship)*, "key plank[s] in the intellectual culture
of sixteenth-century Europe." Cicero was the main

republican figure from the last days of the republic; although only a minor character in the play, his refusal to join the conspirators "shows how their actions, however they are presented, are at odds with the proper goals of the republic." Through their secrecy, manipulation of friendship, contempt for the citizenry, and favoring of violence over the art of persuasion as the new form of political argument, Brutus and Cassius taint healthy republican institutions and values. Even Antony's "Now let it work. Mischief, thou art afoot; / Take thou what course thou wilt" (3.2.275–76) demonstrates his willingness to use his friendship with Caesar and gift for public oratory ("the central feature of the republic at its height") to "help destroy the republic, continuing the civil wars that signalled its decline into dictatorship."

Hapgood, Robert. "Speak Hands for Me: Gesture as Language in *Julius Caesar.*" *Drama Survey* 5 (1966): 162–70. Reprinted in *Essays in Shakespearean Criticism*, edited by James L. Calderwood and Harold E. Toliver, pp. 415–22. Englewood Cliffs, N.J.: Prentice-Hall, 1970.

Hapgood examines Shakespeare's use of nonverbal elements (props, gestures, stage pictures) in *Julius Caesar*. Such use, according to Hapgood, involves a pattern of reversal in which a gesture, for example, is initially falsified or otherwise "perverted" by characters who thereby render themselves vulnerable to its returning on them with "a 'boomerang' effect." Hapgood notes that "the gesture of stabbing is . . . twisted from its normal significance" by "Brutus' attempt to construe an act of betrayal and assassination into a sacrifice." Then stabbing comes "to rights again" on "the battlefield, with its straightforward swordplay," and again in the suicides of Cassius and Brutus, the latter of whom "*runs on* his sword." Hapgood interprets this gestural pattern as a suppression of spontaneous, direct expression and sees in this "a mordant critique of the Roman way of life."

Kahn, Coppélia. "Mettle and Melting Spirits in *Julius Caesar.*" Chapter 4 in *Roman Shakespeare: Warriors, Wounds, and Women*, pp. 77–109. London: Routledge, 1997.

Focusing on the wound as "a fetish of Roman masculinity," Kahn draws on feminist and psychoanalytic criticism to "interrogate . . . the gender ideologies that uphold Roman *virtus*" (i.e., Roman manliness—martial, valorous, and self-disciplined) in *Lucrece, Titus Andronicus, Julius Caesar, Antony and Cleopatra, Coriolanus,* and *Cymbeline.* In the chapter *on Julius Caesar*, Kahn examines Brutus's encounters with Cassius (1.2) and Portia (2.1) in order to chart his evolution as "exemplar of Roman *virtus.*" The two meetings demonstrate how the ethos of Roman manliness was (1) rooted in rivalrous emulation and (2) implicated in the feminine. Cassius's seduction of Brutus "from passivity to political action" mirrors for Brutus "the public Roman," thereby confirming masculine identity; Portia's failure to draw a secret from her husband captures his divided interior (the " 'feminine' Other within him"), thus subverting masculine identity. The crucial sexual difference in the play, however, is not "framed simply as one between male and female." In the orchard scene, we hear of Portia's "voluntary wound . . . in the thigh" (2.1.323–24), a valorous gesture of emulation that serves to idealize the masculine constructs of Roman *virtus* while also destabilizing traditional distinctions between *polis* (the public/political forum of men) and *oikos* (the private/domestic household of women, children, and slaves). Portia's act "shows . . . a fine discernment in this strategy of constructing herself as a man, for . . . men mutually confirm their identities as Roman through bonds with each other. Brutus can trust Portia only as a man." As the wounded bodies of Portia and Caesar manifest— his being "the feminized object through which the conspirators try to restore their manly virtue as citizens of the republic"—the wound that signifies *virtus* cannot be equated with a fixed and delimited masculinity, neatly and rigidly separated from the feminine; though rendered subordinate and inferior, women are essential to the "construction of male subjects as Roman." Roman masculinity in Shakespeare remains a "question of sexual difference—an open question, still."

Marshall, Cynthia. "Shakespeare, Crossing the Rubicon." *Shakespeare Survey* 53 (2000): 73–88.

Marshall combines source study with psychoanalytic criticism to explore the semiotics of character in *Julius Caesar* and *Coriolanus*. Prompted by the question "What are dramatic characters characterizations of?" she examines Shakespeare's use of Plutarch's *Lives* (see below), the primary source of his Roman plays and a "key text in the evolution of the early modern concept of character or subjectivity," to argue that in refiguring narrative as drama, Shakespeare establishes "our culture's prevailing model of character as one that is at once intensely performative and putatively interiorized." Plutarch's emphasis on internal debate in his narration of Caesar's Rubicon dilemma and the Oedipal dream that resolves it—an episode not found in Shakespeare—focuses Marshall's analysis of how Shakespeare converts decision making into dramatic event in two scenes *of Julius Caesar*: Brutus's struggle as he considers whether to join the conspiracy (2.1) and Caesar's decision to go forth on the ides of March (2.2). The first is interiorized by the use of "soliloquy-as-dialogue" (2.1.10–36, 51–61, 64–72, and 84–93); the second exteriorized by assigning two opposing interpretations of a dream, further differentiated as male and female, to Decius Brutus and Calphurnia, with Caesar ultimately transferring his fears to his wife (2.2.110). Brutus's articulation of his moral ambivalence in a dialogic soliloquy that internalizes his struggle results in an "unprecedented depth of character" that "accords with the intrinsic importance of moral sensibility to Western culture's basic idea of selfhood." Detecting a trace of Plutarch's interiorized Rubicon decision in *Julius Caesar*, Marshall claims that Shakespeare "had to cross this symbolic Rubicon, marking off the richly inventive but largely plot-driven plays of the 1590s from the deeply characterological dramas that follow, in order to take possession of his territory as a dramatist."

Miles, Gary. "How Roman Are Shakespeare's Romans?" *Shakespeare Quarterly* 40 (1989): 257–83.

Writing as a classicist, Miles compares Shakespeare's Roman characters to depictions of these characters in the writings and sculpture of their own times. He finds significant and interesting differences between Romans and Shakespeare's Romans. For the Romans themselves, character was defined entirely by public action—by holding public offices, by winning military victories, and by providing public benefactions. Shakespeare, though, establishes his Roman characters—at least partly because of the influence of his main source, Plutarch's *Lives* (see below)—in terms of "essentially personal values and intentions." For example, both Antony and the play *Julius Caesar* force us to reflect on the extent to which Brutus is an honorable man, that is, the extent to which his inner character is consistent with his conduct. Although the Romans had in the word *honorabilis* a cognate for Shakespeare's *honorable*, the Latin word has reference only to one's outer condition and political position and therefore would not give rise to reflections on the interior lives of Romans themselves. Miles emphasizes that he does not mean to say that Shakespeare regards the public lives of his Roman characters as trivial or irrelevant or that the Romans themselves were two-dimensional and uninteresting. Rather he calls attention to the changes in worldview and language between classical Rome and Shakespeare's England.

Paster, Gail Kern. " 'In the Spirit of Men There Is No Blood': Blood as Trope of Gender in *Julius Caesar*." *Shakespeare Quarterly* 40 (1989): 284–98. Revised and reprinted as part of *The Body Embarrassed: Drama and Disciplines of Shame in Early Modern England*, pp. 93–111. New York: Cornell University Press, 1993.

In an ambitious project of historical reconstruction, Paster deciphers the "complex annotation of gender difference in apparently unambiguously gendered characters." Through an interrogation of Shakespeare's use of blood and bleeding in *Julius Caesar*, Paster concludes that the outbreak of war after Caesar's assassination results from the disclosure of his wounds, a disclosure that draws attention to the bleeding body, which had specific cultural meanings in early modern Europe. As Paster shows, in *Julius Caesar* "the meaning of blood and bleeding becomes part of an insistent rhetoric of bodily conduct in which the bleeding body signifies a shameful token of uncontrol, as a failure of physical self-mastery particularly associated with woman."

Plutarch. "The Life of Julius Caesar," "The Life of Antonius," "The Life of Brutus." In *Lives of the Noble Grecians and Romans*, trans. Thomas North. In *Selected Lives of the Noble Grecians and Romans*, edited by Paul

Turner, 2:1–46, 104–61, 162–97. 2 vols. Carbondale: Southern Illinois University Press, 1963.

Plutarch chronologically traces the characters and careers of individual men, filling his accounts with anecdotes illustrating their traits. Sir Thomas North's 1579 translation was Shakespeare's main source for *Julius Caesar*, for which he drew on all three of the Lives listed above. For example, from "The Life of Julius Caesar" he took the names of the tribunes Flavius and Marullus and their 1.1 confrontation with the plebeians over the adorning of Caesar's statues. The 1.3 descriptions of the marvels visible in the streets also come from "The Life of Caesar." Both it and "The Life of Brutus" gave Shakespeare detailed accounts of Caesar's 3.1 assassination and of the events immediately surrounding it. The scene in which Antony, Lepidus, and Octavius meet to determine whom they will proscribe (4.1) draws on "The Life of Antonius." For the quarrel between Brutus and Cassius (4.3) and for the details of the Battle of Philippi (Act 5) Shakespeare turned to "The Life of Brutus," which also provided the episodes in the domestic life of Brutus and Portia that he vividly dramatized.

Rabkin, Norman. "Structure, Convention, and Meaning in *Julius Caesar*." *Journal of English and Germanic Philology* 63 (1964): 240–54. Revised and reprinted as part of "The Polity" in *Shakespeare and the Common Understanding*, pp. 105–19 (of 80–149). New York: Free Press, 1967.

Rabkin focuses on the first two scenes of the play's second act, 2.1 set in Brutus's home, 2.2 in Caesar's, the night before the assassination. First examining the structure of these scenes, Rabkin finds them remarkably similar. Just as 2.1 begins with Brutus, his sleep disturbed, calling out for a servant, so 2.2 begins with Caesar, unable to sleep, calling out. In the course of each scene, each man welcomes the conspirators as a group of honored friends, each is supplicated by his wife on her knees, and each exits on his way to the Capitol. These structural parallels highlight other similarities between the two men's characters—their stoicism, their occasional bluster, their use of "fine rhetoric to support a mistaken decision." For Rabkin, they are both "flawed giants," and these parallels discredit Brutus's version of the assassination as an act of public virtue. Rabkin also identifies Antony's speech in the Forum as a moment of transformation in dramatic convention, shifting the play from a tragical history to a revenge tragedy, casting Brutus now in the role of "first criminal" and Antony simultaneously as the hero-revenger and "the villain of the piece." With this shift Brutus's character undergoes degeneration, "which demonstrates clearly that even character is determined more by process than by abiding and shaping inner principles."

Ripley, John. *"Julius Caesar" on Stage in England and America, 1599–1973*. Cambridge: Cambridge University Press, 1980.

In this extensive and detailed stage history of *Julius Caesar*, Ripley draws on archival materials (e.g., promptbooks, reviews, diaries, letters, and interviews) to reconstruct Anglo-American productions from 1599 to 1973. The volume begins with a brief overview of the afterlife of *Julius Caesar* in criticism and on stage and concludes with an afterword offering some directions for future exploration. Ripley moves quickly through seventeenth- and eighteenth-century productions to concentrate on major nineteenth-century revivals under the following chapter headings: "John P. Kemble, 1812," "From Young to Phelps, 1819–65," "The Booth-Barrett-Davenport era," "The Meiningen Court

Company (1881) and Beerbohm Tree (1898)," and "F. R. Benson at Stratford-upon-Avon (1892–1915)." Separate chapters deal with American revivals in the intervals 1770–1870 and 1892–1949; the final chapters cover the efforts of William Bridges-Adams at Stratford-upon-Avon (1919–34), productions in London between 1900 and 1949, and stagings in England and North America from 1950 to 1973. For each reconstruction, Ripley tries to determine what text was spoken; records distribution of speeches, cast size, cuts, and (more rarely) additions; considers the particular theater and audience tastes; and describes set design, costumes, stage business, crowd scenes, and the interpretation of the four major roles (Caesar, Brutus, Cassius, and Antony). The play has enjoyed perennial popularity on the stage from its first performance at the Globe in 1599, and this despite "grave theatrical drawbacks": a titular hero who dies in Act 3; a three-way competition for the audience's sympathy by Cassius, Brutus, and Antony; a mob that can either rob the play of vitality if it is too small or inactive or "swamp . . . the action" if given to boisterous spectacle; the threat of anticlimax in the final two acts; and "little feminine interest." The prevailing assessment of the play in the eighteenth and nineteenth centuries that it is successful only in its parts gave way in the twentieth century to recognition of its wholeness "and a willingness on the part of the theatre to offer more than piecemeal solutions to its problems."

Stirling, Brents. " 'Or Else Were This a Savage Spectacle.' " In *Unity in Shakespearean Tragedy*. New York: Columbia University Press, 1956, pp. 40–54. Reprinted in *Essays in Shakespearean Criticism*, edited by James L. Calderwood and Harold E. Toliver, pp. 405–14. Englewood Cliffs, N.J.: Prentice-Hall, 1970.

Stirling catalogues the pervasiveness of ritual and ceremony in *Julius Caesar*, which includes the dressing of Caesar's statues in 1.1; the "feast of Lupercal" in 1.2, together with the formal entries and exits of Caesar and his train, and the offstage ceremony of the crown offering; the augury of 2.2; the ceremonial kneeling before Caesar of each of the conspirators who surround him before the assassination, their each stabbing him in their turn (Casca first and Brutus last), and their ritualized bathing of their arms in his blood (3.1). Stirling determines that Brutus's incorporation of the assassination into the pattern of Roman ritual is motivated largely by his attempt—by depersonalizing Caesar and the conspirators—to assuage the contradiction inherent in an idealized conspiracy that in the main satisfies Brutus's personal ends. Stirling then goes on to examine Antony's strategy of appropriating Brutus's ritualization of the assassination through his own counterrituals—Antony's shaking each of the conspirators' bloody hands in turn, just as they stabbed Caesar in turn, and Antony's display of Caesar's mantle to the Roman mob, assigning each rent in the garment to the stroke of a particular conspirator's sword. Thereby Antony undoes Brutus's version of the assassination as a sacrifice and transforms it into the butchery of Caesar-as-prey by the conspirators-as-hunters.

Zander, Horst, ed. *Julius Caesar: New Critical Essays*. London: Routledge, 2005.

This collection consists of twenty new essays spanning a variety of critical issues and ideologies. The essays are as follows: Martin Jehne, "History's Alternative Caesars: *Julius Caesar* and Current Historiography"; Clifford Ronan, "Caesar On and Off the Renaissance English Stage"; Vivian Thomas, "Shakespeare's Sources: Translations, Transformations, and Intertextuality in *Julius Caesar*"; Barbara L. Parker, "From Monarchy to Tyranny: *Julius Caesar* among Shakespeare's Roman Works"; Joseph Candido, " 'Time . . . Come Round': Plot Construction in *Julius Caesar*"; Barbara J. Baines, " 'That every like is not the same': The Vicissitudes of Language in *Julius Caesar*"; J. L. Simmons, "From Theatre to Globe: The Construction of Character in *Julius Caesar*"; Naomi Conn Liebler, "Buying and Selling So(u)les: Marketing Strategies and the Politics of Performance in *Julius Caesar*"; Andreas Mahler, " 'There is restitution, no end of restitution, only not for us': Experimental Tragedy and the Early Modern Subject in *Julius Caesar*"; David Hawkes, "Shakespeare's *Julius Caesar*: Marxist and Post-Marxist Approaches"; David Willbern, "Constructing Caesar: A Psychoanalytic Reading"; Simon Barker, " 'It's an actor, boss. Unarmed': The Rhetoric of *Julius Caesar*"; Dennis Kezar, "*Julius Caesar*'s Analogue Clock and the Accents of History"; Graham Holderness and Marcus Nevitt, "Major among the Minors: A Cultural Materialist Reading *of Julius Caesar*"; Coppélia Kahn, " 'Passions of some difference': Friendship and Emulation in *Julius Caesar*"; James Rigney, "Stage Worlds of *Julius Caesar*: Theatrical Features and Their History"; Michael Anderegg, "Orson Welles and After: *Julius Caesar* and Twentieth Century Totalitarianism"; Tom Matheson, "Royal *Caesar*"; Michael Greenwald, "Multicultural and Regendered Romans: *Julius Caesar* in North America, 1969–2000"; and Mariangela Tempera, "Political Caesar: *Julius Caesar* on the Italian Stage." The editor's introductory essay identifies main critical issues, charts the critical reception of the play through the twentieth century, analyzes various theoretical and ideological approaches to *Julius Caesar,* and provides a selective account of the play on stage and in film, on television, and in other media. Among the issues Zander addresses are the question of the play's protagonist, the play's temporal and spatial design, and the private Caesar versus the public institution of "Caesar." Zander claims that *Julius Caesar* marks the turning point in the Shakespeare canon, signaling the "shift from history to basic issues of human existence."

Shakespeare's Language

Abbott, E. A. *A Shakespearian Grammar.* New York: Haskell House, 1972.

This compact reference book, first published in 1870, helps with many difficulties in Shakespeare's language. It systematically accounts for a host of differences between Shakespeare's usage and sentence structure and our own.

Blake, Norman. *Shakespeare's Language: An Introduction.* New York: St. Martin's Press, 1983.

This general introduction to Elizabethan English discusses various aspects of the language of Shakespeare and his contemporaries, offering possible meanings for hundreds of ambiguous constructions.

Hope, Jonathan. *Shakespeare's Grammar.* London: Arden Shakespeare, 2003.

Commissioned as a replacement for Abbott's *Shakespearian Grammar,* Hope's book is organized in terms of the two basic parts of speech, the noun and the verb. After extensive analysis of the noun phrase and the verb phrase come briefer discussions of subjects and agents, objects, complements, and adverbials.

Houston, John. *Shakespearean Sentences: A Study in Style and Syntax.* Baton Rouge: Louisiana State University Press, 1988.

Houston studies Shakespeare's stylistic choices, considering matters such as sentence length and the relative positions of subject, verb, and direct object. Examining plays throughout the canon in a roughly chronological, developmental order, he analyzes how sentence structure is used in setting tone, in characterization, and for other dramatic purposes.

Onions, C. T. *A Shakespeare Glossary.* Oxford: Clarendon Press, 1986.

This revised edition updates Onions's standard, selective glossary of words and phrases in Shakespeare's plays that are now obsolete, archaic, or obscure.

Robinson, Randal. *Unlocking Shakespeare's Language: Help for the Teacher and Student.* Urbana, Ill.: National Council of Teachers of English and the ERIC Clearinghouse on Reading and Communication Skills, 1989.

Specifically designed for the high-school and undergraduate college teacher and student, Robinson's book addresses the problems that most often hinder present-day readers of Shakespeare. Through work with his own students, Robinson found that many readers today are particularly puzzled by such stylistic characteristics as subject-verb inversion, interrupted structures, and compression. He shows how our own colloquial language contains comparable structures, and thus helps students recognize such structures when they find them in Shakespeare's plays. This book supplies work sheets—with examples from major plays—to illuminate and remedy such problems as unusual sequences of words and the separation of related parts of sentences.

Williams, Gordon. *A Dictionary of Sexual Language and Imagery in Shakespearean and Stuart Literature.* 3 vols. London: Athlone Press, 1994.

Williams provides a comprehensive list of words to which Shakespeare, his contemporaries, and later Stuart writers gave sexual meanings. He supports his identification of these meanings by extensive quotations.

Shakespeare's Life

Baldwin, T. W. *William Shakspere's Petty School.* Urbana: University of Illinois Press, 1943.

Baldwin here investigates the theory and practice of the petty school, the first level of education in Elizabethan England. He focuses on that educational system primarily as it is reflected in Shakespeare's art.

Baldwin, T. W. *William Shakspere's Small Latine and Lesse Greeke.* 2 vols. Urbana: University of Illinois Press, 1944.

Baldwin attacks the view that Shakespeare was an uneducated genius—a view that had been dominant among Shakespeareans since the eighteenth century. Instead, Baldwin shows, the educational system of Shakespeare's time would have given the playwright a strong background in the classics, and there is much in the plays that shows how Shakespeare benefited from such an education.

Beier, A. L., and Roger Finlay, eds. *London 1500–1700: The Making of the Metropolis.* New York: Longman, 1986.

Focusing on the economic and social history of early modern London, these collected essays probe aspects of metropolitan life, including "Population and Disease," "Commerce and Manufacture," and "Society and Change."

Bentley, G. E. *Shakespeare's Life: A Biographical Handbook*. New Haven: Yale University Press, 1961.

This "just-the-facts" account presents the surviving documents of Shakespeare's life against an Elizabethan background.

Cressy, David. *Education in Tudor and Stuart England*. London: Edward Arnold, 1975.

This volume collects sixteenth-, seventeenth-, and early eighteenth-century documents detailing aspects of formal education in England, such as the curriculum, the control and organization of education, and the education of women.

Dutton, Richard. *William Shakespeare: A Literary Life*. New York: St. Martin's Press, 1989.

Not a biography in the traditional sense, Dutton's very readable work nevertheless "follows the contours of Shakespeare's life" as he examines Shakespeare's career as playwright and poet, with consideration of his patrons, theatrical associations, and audience.

Honan, Park. *Shakespeare: A Life*. New York: Oxford University Press, 1998.

Honan's accessible biography focuses on the various contexts of Shakespeare's life—physical, social, political, and cultural—to place the dramatist within a lucidly described world. The biography includes detailed examinations of, for example, Stratford schooling, theatrical politics of 1590s London, and the careers of Shakespeare's associates. The author draws on a wealth of established knowledge and on interesting new research into local records and documents; he also engages in speculation about, for example, the possibilities that Shakespeare was a tutor in a Catholic household in the north of England in the 1580s and that he played particular roles in his own plays, areas that reflect new, but unproven and debatable, data—though Honan is usually careful to note where a particular narrative "has not been capable of proof or disproof."

Schoenbaum, S. *William Shakespeare: A Compact Documentary Life.* New York: Oxford University Press, 1977.

This standard biography economically presents the essential documents from Shakespeare's time in an accessible narrative account of the playwright's life.

Shakespeare's Theater

Bentley, G. E. *The Profession of Player in Shakespeare's Time, 1590–1642.* Princeton: Princeton University Press, 1984.

Bentley readably sets forth a wealth of evidence about performance in Shakespeare's time, with special attention to the relations between player and company, and the business of casting, managing, and touring.

Berry, Herbert. *Shakespeare's Playhouses.* New York: AMS Press, 1987.

Berry's six essays collected here discuss (with illustrations) varying aspects of the four playhouses in which Shakespeare had a financial stake: the Theatre in Shoreditch, the Blackfriars, and the first and second Globe.

Berry, Herbert, William Ingram, and Glynne Wickham, eds. *English Professional Theatre, 1530–1660.* Cambridge: Cambridge University Press, 2000.

Wickham presents the government documents designed to control professional players, their plays, and playing places. Ingram handles the professional actors, giving as representative a life of the actor Augustine Phillips, and discussing, among other topics, patrons, acting companies, costumes, props, playbooks, provincial playing, and child actors. Berry treats the twenty-three different London playhouses from 1560 to 1660 for which there are records, including four inns.

Cook, Ann Jennalie. *The Privileged Playgoers of Shakespeare's London.* Princeton: Princeton University Press, 1981.

Cook's work argues, on the basis of sociological, economic, and documentary evidence, that Shakespeare's audience—and the audience for English Renaissance drama generally—consisted mainly of the "privileged."

Greg, W. W. *Dramatic Documents from the Elizabethan Playhouses.* 2 vols. Oxford: Clarendon Press, 1931.

Greg itemizes and briefly describes almost all the play manuscripts that survive from the period 1590 to around 1660, including, among other things, players' parts. His second volume offers facsimiles of selected manuscripts.

Gurr, Andrew. *Playgoing in Shakespeare's London.* 3rd ed. Cambridge: Cambridge University Press, 2004.

Gurr charts how the theatrical enterprise developed from its modest beginnings in the late 1560s to become a thriving institution in the 1600s. He argues that there were important changes over the period 1567–1644 in the playhouses, the audience, and the plays.

Harbage, Alfred. *Shakespeare's Audience.* New York: Columbia University Press, 1941.

Harbage investigates the fragmentary surviving evidence to interpret the size, composition, and behavior of Shakespeare's audience.

Hattaway, Michael. *Elizabethan Popular Theatre: Plays in Performance.* London: Routledge & Kegan Paul, 1982.

Beginning with a study of the popular drama of the late Elizabethan age—a description of the stages, performance conditions, and acting of the period—this volume concludes with an analysis of five well-known plays of the 1590s, one of them (*Titus Andronicus*) by Shakespeare.

Shapiro, Michael. *Children of the Revels: The Boy Companies of Shakespeare's Time and Their Plays.* New York: Columbia University Press, 1977.

Shapiro chronicles the history of the amateur and quasi-professional child companies that flourished in London at the end of Elizabeth's reign and the beginning of James's.

The Publication of Shakespeare's Plays

Blayney, Peter W. M. *The First Folio of Shakespeare.* Hanover, Md.: Folger, 1991.

Blayney's accessible account of the printing and later life of the First Folio—an amply illustrated catalogue to a 1991 Folger Shakespeare Library exhibition—analyzes the mechanical production of the First Folio, describing how the Folio was made, by whom and for whom, how much it cost, and its ups and downs (or, rather, downs and ups) since its printing in 1623.

Hinman, Charlton. *The Norton Facsimile: The First Folio of Shakespeare.* 2nd ed. New York: W. W. Norton, 1996.

This facsimile presents a photographic reproduction of an "ideal" copy of the First Folio of Shakespeare; Hinman attempts to represent each page in its most fully corrected state. This second edition includes an important new introduction by Peter W. M. Blayney.

Hinman, Charlton. *The Printing and Proof-Reading of the First Folio of Shakespeare.* 2 vols. Oxford: Clarendon Press, 1963.

In the most arduous study of a single book ever undertaken, Hinman attempts to reconstruct how the Shakespeare First Folio of 1623 was set into type and run off the press, sheet by sheet. He also provides almost all the known variations in readings from copy to copy.

Key to
Famous Lines and Phrases

Beware the ides of March.   [*Soothsayer*—1.2.21]

. . . he doth bestride the narrow world
Like a Colossus, and we petty men
Walk under his huge legs and peep about
To find ourselves dishonorable graves.
                        [*Cassius*—1.2.142–45]

The fault, dear Brutus, is not in our stars,
But in ourselves[.]   [*Cassius*—1.2.147–48]

Upon what meat doth this our Caesar feed
That he is grown so great?   [*Cassius*—1.2.158–59]

Let me have men about me that are fat[.]
                            [*Caesar*—1.2.202]

But for mine own part, it was Greek to me.
                        [*Casca*—1.2.294–95]

Cowards die many times before their deaths;
The valiant never taste of death but once.
                        [*Caesar*—2.2.34–35]

            Danger knows full well
That Caesar is more dangerous than he.
We are two lions littered in one day,
And I the elder and more terrible.
                        [*Caesar*—2.2.47–50]

Know: Caesar doth not wrong, nor without cause
Will he be satisfied.   [*Caesar*—3.1.52–53]

Et tu, Brutè?—Then fall, Caesar.   [*Caesar*—3.1.85]

O mighty Caesar, dost thou lie so low?
Are all thy conquests, glories, triumphs, spoils
Shrunk to this little measure? [*Antony*—3.1.164–66]

Thou art the ruins of the noblest man
That ever livèd in the tide of times.
                              [*Antony*—3.1.282–83]

Cry "Havoc!" and let slip the dogs of war[.]
                              [*Antony*—3.1.299]

Romans, countrymen, and lovers, hear me for my
cause[.]   [*Brutus*—3.2.14–15]

Friends, Romans, countrymen, lend me your ears.
I come to bury Caesar, not to praise him.
The evil that men do lives after them;
The good is oft interrèd with their bones.
                              [*Antony*—3.2.82–85]

Ambition should be made of sterner stuff.
                              [*Antony*—3.2.101]

O judgment, thou art fled to brutish beasts,
And men have lost their reason!
                              [*Antony*—3.2.114–15]

This was the most unkindest cut of all.
                              [*Antony*—3.2.195]

There is a tide in the affairs of men
Which, taken at the flood, leads on to fortune[.]
                              [*Brutus*—4.3.249–50]

O Julius Caesar, thou art mighty yet;
Thy spirit walks abroad and turns our swords
In our own proper entrails.   [*Brutus*—5.3.105–7]

This was the noblest Roman of them all. . . .
His life was gentle and the elements
So mixed in him that nature might stand up
And say to all the world "This was a man."
                           [*Antony*—5.5.74, 79–81]

NOW AVAILABLE—THE FOLGER LUMINARY SHAKESPEARE IOS APP

An interactive reading experience that enriches the Folger Shakespeare editions.

Explore the digital edition of the gold-standard play text.

AVAILABLE NOW:

Coming soon: *Richard III* and *Julius Caesar*

INTERACTIVE FEATURES:

Audio
- Includes a full-length audio recording of the play performed by professional Shakespearean actors.

Learning Tools
- Richly annotated image galleries, videos, and multimedia enhance the reading experience.

Commentary
- Includes short, accessible commentaries on key moments in the play written by the world's leading Shakespearean scholars and performers.

Connect
- Publish private commentaries within the app and on devices of students and colleagues.

- Take and share notes using student groups or social media.

To find out more and see a demonstration of the app.
visit **Pages.SimonandSchuster.com/FolgerLuminaryApp**